THE Sea Slave

A True Story

Kyle Matthews

First Edition

NEWMAN SPRINGS PUBLISHING
320 Broad Street
Red Bank, NJ 07701

First originally published by Newman Springs Publishing 2024

ISBN 979-8-89061-264-9 (Paperback)
ISBN 979-8-89061-265-6 (Digital)

Printed in the United States of America

I was told once by a psychiatrist that I had to write down on paper all the things in my past that haunted me today. Things that I thought were normal were inhumane acts that were wrong! After I wrote everything I could think of, I kept going through my life. I have God in my life today! I give all my thanks to his glory, to break free from the chains that were holding me in bondage.

The only way God will start forgiving me is if I start forgiving other people. But most of all, I should start forgiving myself!

The year was 1986, the dead of winter. I'll never forget it as long as I live! I was at Friendly's with a friend whose father owned an offshore lobster boat. He had invited me out to lunch. I was basically broke, and he was buying.

After the meal, Jimmy pulled out a wad of cash that was way too big for a wallet to hold. My eyes bulged, and I asked where he got all that money! Jimmy said, "I got the money busting my ass lugging lobster traps around all week long."

I did not care about the parts "busting ass" or "lugging traps around all day." The wad of money blocked all that out. So I asked him if I could get a job. Jimmy (now deceased) said, "We have a full crew on my dad's boat. I know of someone that will hire you. His name is Ron Howard." And he chuckled a little bit.

I was so excited. "How can I get a hold of him?"

Jimmy rolled his phone number off his tongue like nothing. He said, "Tell him I told you to call and that he hires greenhorns [greenhorn: new guy]."

All I remember was being so excited. My brother and I used to go down to the docks in Woods Hole in Cape Cod when we were kids. We would look at all the fishing boats getting ready for an adventure out to sea, and we would talk about going out on a fishing boat one day.

I was so happy, I couldn't wait to go home and call Ron Howard. As soon as I got home, I ran to the phone to call this man who hired greenhorns.

Ron Howard picked up the phone. He was very mild mannered and polite. "Hello, this is Ron Howard."

And I replied, "Ron, this is Kyle Matthews. Jimmy had me call you for a site on the *Barnacle*. He said you hire greenhorns!"

Ron Howard laughed out loud and said, "I sure do." He asked me if I could meet him at Dickey's Wharf in Hyannis.

"I sure can. When do you want to meet me?" I asked with anticipation.

"How about if you meet me this Saturday morning 5:00 a.m."

I said, "Great. I'll see you there."

Oh boy. I remember the excitement I had felt with my heart pounding. I was about to be an offshore lobsterman! There was not a single soul I didn't tell. Everyone I knew and some I didn't even know knew.

The big day came to go fishing. I was eighteen years old at the time and didn't own a car, so I got a ride from my sister's friend Teddy. We got there real early so I wouldn't miss this Ron Howard. I remember walking to the boat, and it was so cold, my eyelashes were freezing together from my watering eyes.

I look back now that I'm fifty-seven years old and realize that you don't have much fear—or any fear for that matter—when you're younger, or maybe you're just stupid. Whatever the case may be, I was going to be an offshore lobsterman.

When I got to the boat, there were three men on deck (the back of the boat where the lobster traps are stacked). The men did not say one word to me. They were just staring at me with blank expressions on their faces.

Then a man came out of the wheelhouse (where you steer the boat and keep watch for other boats). "Hi, my name is Howard. Are you Kyle?"

"Yes, sir. I am looking for a job."

He said aloud, "How old are you?"

I replied, "I'm 18 years old."

He got all excited. "That's when I went offshore lobstering with my dad, who was Steve Howard that owned a swordfish and lobster boat. He was excited to have me aboard. All I could smell was diesel fuel and fish." Ron asked if I could go on the next trip. "We need a body to fill in and another for a full time sight. How about if you make this trip and see how you like it?"

I said "great" with so much excitement, he laughed aloud. Ron said he was going to take the trip off and that Nick (the first mate) was taking the boat as captain this trip. Then there would be Paul, the Buster, Connor, and me, Kyle.

He brought me to the wheelhouse window and pointed to the Buster and Connor. I guess Paul wasn't there. The Buster had long curly reddish brown hair, blue eyes, and big hands. He was just big. He didn't have one nice line on his face. It was one long snarl and a mean look, like he hated life and some!

Connor was different. He had short black hair and wore brown khakis. He was wide-eyed. Connor (deceased) was of average height (six feet). He had a good size to him with a smile from ear to ear.

Ron said the boat would be leaving in two or three days, and we'd be gone for five to six days, depending on the weather. Ron asked if I had any oilskins or any foul-weather gear. (Years ago, before we had waterproof rain jackets, the men would smear tar on their clothing to waterproof themselves from the rain and sea spray, so that's how rain gear got the nickname *oilskins*.)

I said no and asked Ron where I could get some foul-weather gear.

He wasn't from around here. "I'm from the North. And Chatham, Cape Cod, is a little too far from here also. But try Salty Point Marine in Plymouth."

I was so relieved because I lived in Plymouth, Massachusetts.

As I left the wheelhouse to go on deck, the blast of cold air made my eyes water. It was so cold. I heard Ron Howard say, "I'll call you in two days to let you know when the boat is leaving. Thanks." He was smiling at me like he had won the lottery or something.

As I climbed on the dock, I heard somebody say, "He'll never make it." It didn't bother me any; I wanted it badly! I remember not even turning around to see who said it, and the cold wind was also biting on my back.

I was so excited, I remember forgetting to give Howard my telephone number. I remember worrying about that all the way home like it was yesterday.

Teddy calmed me down halfway home and said, "Just call him and leave your number on his answering machine."

As soon as I got home, I called and left my telephone number and thanked him for letting me try out this job.

The next thing I had to worry about was rain gear. I didn't have much money. I called my father and asked him if he could help me. He took me to the store and bought me some warm-weather gear while cursing me, "Why do you want to be a fisherman!" My father was a schoolteacher, and he always told me, "Make your avocation your vocation." So I did. My brother-in-law John lent me his boots and oilskins, and I was all set and ready to be an offshore lobsterman.

Jimmy had already left on his father's offshore lobster boat, and I only had one more day left before I would go fishing. I remember my brother Antonio was excited for me. He was looking forward to eating some lobster. I was the youngest of eight siblings: four boys and four girls. Antonio and I were the closest, seeing as he was next to the youngest, me.

That evening, I remember staring at the phone and waiting for it to ring, my heart fluttering with anticipation. You ever heard this saying? "Don't stare at a pot of water on the stove. If you're trying to make it boil, it won't boil."

When Ron finally called, it was late. I remember him being so nice, apologizing for calling so late. The boat was leaving the next day, and Ron wanted everybody to be there early: 5:00 a.m. sharp!

I didn't sleep very well. I remember being nervous and had butterflies in my stomach. I remember my mom telling me that I was going to be somebody special one day. She always told me that.

Teddy was already there at the kitchen table before I even got downstairs, yelling at me, "You're going to be late. Let's go!"

I had all my clothes packed and ready to go. My sister-in-law let me use her father's air force duffel bag, which he used in the service.

Jimmy had told me, "Whatever you do, don't bring a suitcase. Ron is very superstitious and might not bring you. He thinks it is bad luck!"

I remember being so proud that day. I hugged my mom goodbye and said, "I'll bring you home some money, Mom!"

When I arrived at the boat, it was dark out still. I was real early and very happy about that.

Teddy pulled in backward to the dock to unload my gear so I didn't have to walk forty to fifty yards away from the parking lot.

Somebody was on the boat, and I didn't recognize him. He came out of the wheelhouse. "Are you Paul or Kyle?"

I told him I was Kyle, and I asked if he was Nick (deceased now). He was real nice to me. He had a beard and dirty-blond graying short hair. Nick wasn't tall (probably five foot seven) and had a good build to him. He was built like a brick shithouse, as the old-timers would say. He was happy to see me and helped me get all my things aboard.

I said goodbye to Teddy and thanked him very much. He didn't want any gas money and wouldn't take any either. He said, "Call me when you get home. You're a good kid. Hang in there." He liked me a lot. He always said, "You're a good kid. Hang in there."

The Nick brought me to the forecastle (the forward part of a ship where the sailors' living quarters are). He threw my bag in a top rack. "This is your rack, top starboard aft rack."

Starboard means right, and *aft* means back. I had no idea what it meant at the time, but it sounded so cool!

I remember Connor coming aboard; he had a black eye and was laughing aloud. Paul was right behind him, bewilderedly looking for a spot to get aboard the boat. I found out earlier that Paul was a greenhorn too (a new guy). I was happy to hear that I was going with another greenhorn. He looked kind and had short curly brown hair and big blue eyes. He was tall, did not have much of a build, and was kind of skinny. I also found out Paul was Ron's brother-in-law.

Paul was also happy that I'd never been on a lobster boat either. Connor was laughing a lot, I remember, to the point of tears in his eyes. He was talking about the bar fight he started at a bar in Wonderland.

I got dressed really warm, ready for the blast of cold air waiting for me outside. Connor said we had a twenty-four-hour steam to the gear 180 nautical miles east-southeast of Nantucket Island, Cape Cod, Massachusetts.

Ron Howard pulled up in a new Chevy pickup truck loaded with three-foot round inflatable orange balls and coils of line (rope). Connor wanted me to stick with him. He said he would take me under his wing. I don't think he liked the fact that Paul was Ron's brother-in-law. It didn't matter to me at all, considering I could be Paul, who was right now stuck with the Buster. He had me cut line into one-fathom pieces (one fathom equals six feet).

There was a small metal box with a cord and plug attached to it. They called it a "hot knife," and that's exactly what it was. It was so cold, it barely cut. And it took forever, it seemed, for how many I had to cut that I don't remember—a lot of them.

Finally, Connor yelled out, "Let's get the hell off this beach!"

Nick yelled out, "Throw all the lines except the forward spring line."

The spring line is attached to a cleat on the starboard side of the boat midship (middle of boat), and then a loop at the other end goes to the dock on a cleat.

I remember being on the bow (the very front of boat). I was so proud and happy, and I was smiling from ear to ear! I waved goodbye to Ron, who was standing on the dock, and I distinctly remember him slowly moving his head left to right and right to left with a big smile on his face.

After Connor showed me how to coil the dock lines and tie them up, Paul and I put the dock lines in the lazaret. The lazaret is in the very back of the boat (called the stern), which you need to open a hatch cover to get in. It is used for storage.

After we put all four dock lines away, Connor wanted us to report back to him. The Buster went inside to cook, and Connor wanted to go over some things with us on the deck.

First, he said I had to secure the deck. Connor was running around like a rabbit, tying things down, laughing, and talking to himself. Connor called us over to the hauler (that's where the line goes to pull the traps off the floor of the ocean). He took us through all four positions. First was railing. You rail the trap and pull your slack. I thought it was a little funny because he was using an imaginary trap! Second position, you're going to middle the trap. They call it *middle* because you're in the middle. The middle man takes the old bait bag full of fish bones out of the trap and puts in a new stuffed bait bag full of redfish. Then you grab the lobster by its back and put it on the sorter table behind you to be banded.

I liked him.

Connor ran off to stack the imaginary lobster trap, which would be third position. Finally, he ran back and said the fourth position was bait and band the lobsters. (For banding, there is a banding tool that opens a half-inch rubber band that you put on the claws so the lobsters won't bite each other in the lobster tank live well.)

"We've already baited bags," he said. "You know how to do that? Let's eat chow."

The smell of diesel fuel and bait was getting stronger and stronger as I sat at the galley table.

I don't remember what we ate on my first trip out, but I do remember not wanting to eat very much.

Connor told me to eat and go right to my rack. We were going to start work as soon as we got to the fishing grounds.

Nick told us he was going to have Connor work with me so he could explain how to take a watch. "Then, Kyle, you wake up the Buster. And the Buster will wake Paul up so Buster can explain watch to Paul, and I'll take last watch so Paul will wake me up. And don't fall asleep! Wake me up for any boats at three miles or if you are in doubt of anything."

It was the first time I'd seen the Nick bark an order and make a wrinkle on his face!

Connor told me to go right to my rack. I listened to his advice.

The forecastle was kind of cold and smelt like fuel from the kerosene stove. The Nick was cursing, lying on the floor. He was trying to light it for the third time, he said.

I finally got to sleep only to be woken up to what felt like a small roller-coaster ride and a tap on the shoulder. "Your watch, Kyle." It was Connor. He still smelled of liquor from the bar fight he had started the night before.

When I got up to the wheelhouse, I felt very queasy. The boat was going forward and aft port to starboard (*starboard* means the right side on a boat), and it seemed like it was happening all at once!

Connor looked at me and said, "If you're going to puke, wait till I tell you how to take watch!"

There were two radars. (A radar is a system for detecting the presence, direction, distance, and speed of aircraft, ships, and other objects by sending out pulses of high-frequency electromagnetic waves that are reflected off the object back to the source.) One radar was set for six miles, and the other radar was set for three miles.

Then there was the loran (a system of long-distance navigation in which position is determined from the intervals between signal pulses received from widely spaced radio transmitters). There were three bars on a small LCD screen. (LCD is the technology used for displays in notebook and other smaller computers.)

He explained of a trim knob. "If the middle bar in the center goes left, turn the knob right at very tiny increments at a time until the bar goes back to the center. And the opposite. If the bars go to the right, turn the knob to the left in small increments till the bar gets back into the middle again. If you have any questions or are in any doubt about anything, wake the Nick up." Then he looked me square in the eyes and said firmly, "Don't fall asleep. Wake somebody up if you can't stay awake."

As soon as he went to the forecastle, I opened the wheelhouse door and got the sickest I've ever been in my entire life. The best way I can describe seasickness is you honestly want to die! Watches were one hour and thirty minutes per man, and it felt like forever and a day! I wasn't looking forward to waking the Buster up, but I was so tired and sick, I didn't even care. As sick as I was, I still remember the proud feeling I had sitting behind the wheel of a steel vessel, steering an offshore lobster boat heading out to sea. Not sure if it was another greenhorn or Paul.

Paul came up from the forecastle like there was a madman pointing a gun at him. His eyes were as wide as silver dollars, and he had one hand over his mouth with liquid squirting out of the cracks of his fingers. I actually felt a little better after looking at Paul.

My first experience waking the Buster up totally sucked! He gave me this ugly and mean snarly look and said, "Get the fuck away from me, sand nigger." I felt sorrier for Paul having the Buster teach him how to take his watch.

When I woke up, I felt rested. I smelled food in the air, and I was very hungry. I heard the Nick screaming in the wheelhouse, "Let's go, men!"

I dressed very warmly, knowing that a cold blast of air was waiting for me! I ate and remember feeling good the first day. As soon as I got on deck, the smell of diesel fuel and bait got my queasiness started all over again. Paul didn't make it that far, but it was a good feeling. Someone else was feeling as bad as I was.

The Buster and Connor were right behind us, putting their foul-weather gear on. Nick was screaming out the wheelhouse window, "Coming up on it."

I had no idea what he was talking about. The weather was nice, I thought, for 180 nautical miles out to sea.

The best way I can describe that first twenty to thirty minutes on deck was total chaos. Connor grabbed this throw grapple (an instrument for catching hold of or seizing something) that was tied to a ten-fathom piece of line that was tied to the boat. He threw it at this tall aluminum pole called a highflier. (It was a twenty-foot aluminum pole with an aluminum hat so the radar can pick it out of the darkness so we can work at night. Then there was a floating device in the middle of the pole and a weight at the bottom of the pole to make it stand up right in the ocean.) Attached to the highflier was a piece of line that extended ten fathoms (sixty feet) to a big orange ball three feet in diameter.

Paul and I watched as they pulled the highflier and ball aboard. Then they put the line in the hauler.

Connor was always calling for me. "Come here, kid!" I guess the Buster took Paul, if you want to call it taking him under his wing.

I was starting off baiting and banding, the Buster was railing, Paul was the middleman, and Connor was staking this first trawl. (A trawl is a mile of line with fifty lobster traps spliced in with a one-fathom piece of line tied to the lobster trap bridle every twenty-five fathoms.)

In the wintertime, Ron had the great idea to put two trawls together so you had one hundred lobster traps and two miles of line. The boat was sixty-five feet long, so you had to stack these wooden traps in order (that weighed one hundred pounds dry) really high just to fit them all on the deck of the boat. The lobster traps were made of solid oak. To fit the whole trawl on deck, you had to stack the traps five high. They called it five high or die!

When I turned around to see how Paul was doing, all I could see was the Buster's big hands and burly long hair like a Viking's. He was grabbing Paul by the shoulders and shaking him like a rag doll, screaming, "Hurry the fuck up, or I'll suck your eye out and fuck your eye socket." Like I said, I'm not sure if it was Paul or another greenhorn? But I know one thing, not one of them came back!

They didn't let me or Paul rail but let us middle, stack, and bait bags. I couldn't get over the fact that I was actually almost two hundred miles offshore lobstering, especially that there were birds out here, big seagulls. They call them blackbacks. Some of them, up high in the sky, looked like eagles. They were so big.

The waves were only one to two feet; they called it light and variable for the wind factor. Connor called it the calm before the storm. Even still, two-feet seas, with the motion of the boat, still have an effect on your stomach, especially after I stacked one hundred traps. At the end of every trawl, I literally felt like I puked my stomach up.

The Buster would scream very loudly, "Puke on your own time!"

Later that day, when the sun was setting, I looked at Paul when we were baiting bags, and I said, "I can't wait till this day ends."

When the sun went down, I started looking forward to dinner and some good sleep.

Connor and Buster would set the gear back out to sea while Paul and I would bait one hundred bait bags as they were setting the gear out. Just before you could barely see anymore, the Nick stuck his head out the wheelhouse window. He said, "The next time you both get a job on a boat?"

We both said "what" at the same time.

He screamed real loud, "Make sure there are no deck lights!"

Flash! The wheelhouse was all lit up. Flash! Then the stern was all lit up. Flash! Then I could see Paul like it was midday, and the Nick was screaming, "Ha ha ha ha ha ha ha!"

Paul and I looked at each other in shock, and then we worked till midnight.

I was so tired, I didn't even want to eat. Connor made me sit at the galley table and eat something.

After three days of being seasick, I was at the galley table literally puking up my food. And being so hungry, I would swallow it back down.

The Nick said to me with a smile, "Sucks when you're seasick and hungry, huh, kid."

That's when I knew I had gained some respect from the Nick.

I remember watching Paul do the dishes. He looked like he was shipwrecked and had washed up on the beach. The sleeves of his oversized sweatshirt were wet and hung down about one foot from his forearms soaking wet. He had pins all over his arms, as did I. Pins were like red holes and pimples all over your wrists and forearms, from the bait juice.

Connor told me to take a pot of boiling water, put some salt in it, and let it dissolve. Then take it off the heat and let it cool (not too much) and dip your hands and wrists in it. We were using whole redfish for lobster bait, and their fins were literally like needles. My hands felt like pincushions (used for holding sewing needles). My fingers were swollen, with pockets of pus in between my fingernails and flesh.

I had last watch, and I couldn't believe at the time: twenty-minute watches. The next day, I could feel the wind getting stronger and colder. The waves were getting bigger—as tall houses. I'm not kidding either. By the next day, the waves were thirty-five to forty-five feet, if not bigger. One minute, you were way up in the sky. Then the next minute, you were down in the valley looking up at a huge wall of water.

Paul was on the back deck with his arms sprawled out, screaming, "We're going to die!"

The Nick asked me what Paul was screaming about. I told him. Nick told me to tell Paul, "Shut the fuck up!"

What I saw was a man full of fear. He thought he was going to die!

Like I said earlier, I wasn't scared when I was younger. You don't have much fear as you do when you get older. I don't think you realize, when you're younger, that you actually can die. I know now what we were in then. It was a nor'easter—not nice! Especially when you're heading home. That's the direction the wind and seas are coming from while you're trying to make your way home, making your way at a snail's pace or as Connor would say, "Let's head for the beach."

The antennas were about two inches in diameter and had at least eight to ten inches of ice built up on them, as well as the mast. You don't want too much ice buildup on the mast. Why? Because the boat will get top-heavy and flip over, and the boat will sink! We were going to have to jog into it (driving the boat really slow into the wind and seas until the weather subsided).

It had been seven or eight days since we left the dock. Paul and I were more excited, and we got some good sleep. My seasickness went away, and the Nick let everyone get some sleep the first day after we hauled all the lobster gear. Then he started watches. When I got up from my deep sleep, I remember there was drool all over my arm, and my pillow was also wet from my drooling.

I overheard Nick talking to Connor about the antenna sheering off from the ice buildup.

Going on the tenth day, it didn't look good; the seas were even worse. I couldn't understand why we were heading southeast. Home was the other way! Now I know why we were going the other way. We had to get closer to the Gulf Stream to warmer water because of the ice building up in the mast.

Back then, they didn't give greenhorns any respect at all! So you learned fast. Well, at least I did, and I didn't ask any questions at all.

Nick said, "We'll deal with it tomorrow." Meaning the antenna, or so I figured out in my mind.

The next day, the weather still seemed awful. Nick asked me to put my gear on. He needed a hand, and I didn't even ask why. I put my boots, pants, and jacket on. When I saw the screwdriver and hose clamps, I knew I had thought right: fix the antenna.

Nick barked out, "Hey, greeny! Follow me."

So I followed Nick to the overhead (the roof of the boat).

Nick had an ice mallet to break the ice every inch of the way. It was like a winter wonderland of ice everywhere, except there were thirty- to forty-foot walls of water on either side of me. The antenna was lying on the overhead, frozen in sea spray about six inches or so. Nick chiseled it out with the screwdriver and made sure the wire was still connected.

I remember Nick tapping my head with the butt end of the screwdriver. "Pay attention to what the hell I am doing instead of bird watching!" I saw a little smile on Nick's face. He positioned the antenna and told me to hold it in place. "And no matter what, don't let go!"

In my mind, I was begging God to let him hurry up before my hands froze to the antenna!

After he was finished, he said, "Good job. Let's go have some hot soup. It's getting fucking cold!"

I'll never forget that!

We finally started heading home after the eleventh day. Years later, Paul told me that Ron actually thought the boat sank after not hearing from us, for what was supposed to be a five-to-six-day trip ended up to be an eleven-to-twelve-day trip. I made $325 in salary. I looked at it like it was good money. My father was a reading teacher, and he made exactly $325 a week in 1986 being a schoolteacher.

When we finally made it back to the dock, Paul and I were so happy. Even the Buster was smiling for the first time in twelve days!

After we unloaded the lobsters, Ron pulled me into the wheelhouse. Ron asked me if I wanted to make another trip. I didn't even hesitate and said yes before I even actually thought about it. Making as much money as my father validated me.

He smiled and said, "Great! We're going to take a few days off to fix a few things. Then we are going to get her [meaning the boat] ready to go fishing again."

That meant bait, fuel, and food for the boat.

Ron said, "The crew will be Connor, Buster, Joe, and me. Nick is taking the trip off, and I'll be taking the boat as captain."

When I got off the boat, Ron asked if I wanted a ride to Plymouth. Ron said, "If you need a ride back to the boat, meet me or the guys on the highway at Exit 6 at the bottom of the ramp in Plymouth."

I was really happy about that because I didn't have any wheels at the time—or a license for that matter. I didn't tell anybody what happened about the bad weather. I lied and said we were so far out to sea, it was nice. I didn't want my mom to worry.

When I ran into Jimmy, he couldn't believe we were out in that storm. It was a bad storm, I found out later. Nor'easters in New England usually are.

*****

The three days I had off went really fast. The next thing I knew, I was standing at Exit 6 at the bottom of the ramp. Ron had called me earlier the previous day to let me know the guys were going to pick me up.

I was waiting at the bottom of the ramp patiently when this red pickup nearly hit me and skidded to a stop! It was Buster, Connor, and Joe, whom I didn't meet yet.

I grabbed my seabag and ran at least thirty yards to the truck. As soon as I got to the truck and I started to throw my seabag in the bed of the truck, the Buster took off really fast so that my seabag would fall on the ground. This time, he pulled at least fifty yards away, and when I got to the truck, the Buster did the same thing. Until I said "fuck it." I was so out of breath and patience! They used to laugh their asses off. Then I'd have to ride in the back of the pickup from Exit 6 in Plymouth to Exit 6 in Hyannis, Cape Cod, Massachusetts (about a forty-five-minute ride in the dead of winter).

Something didn't sit right in my stomach. I did not realize how to listen to my instincts at the time, so I continued the adventure to hell!

When we got to the dock, the Buster got out of the truck and asked, "Are you cold, sand nigger?"

I am part Portuguese and Cape Verdean, so I had a tan complexion.

Joe introduced himself to me. He was handsome with curly black hair and deep blue eyes, and he had a good build to him. He was also Ron's brother-in-law.

There was something I liked about Joe. When you're young, I guess there's something about looking up to somebody that's rough-and-tumble.

Ron showed up with a truckload of food neatly consolidated in cardboard boxes. We had depleted the food from last trip almost completely dry. Ron believed in having a well-stocked boat of food, and now I know why. I was glad to hear that because Buster was a mountain man (at least he looked like one), and I actually had the thought of him eating the weakest one of the crew.

The Nick was on the boat, going over a few things with Ron. I was told to bait my one hundred bags that were tied in the very same spot on the rail, except this time, the bait bags were frozen solid by ice from the freezing sea spray of the heavy seas.

I finished baiting my one hundred bait bags and ate my hot dog and went to my rack. They always ate hot dogs on the ride out. Every time I eat a hot dog, I remember baiting one hundred bait bags. I remember it till this day and probably will for the rest of my life.

Ron always loved to make greenhorns sick on the way out to sea. He would laugh, talking about making creamed salmon and peas on toast for supper. The tradition for lunch on the ride out to sea was always hot dogs and beans, and the ride home was always pasta and sauce.

The ride was nice, which made me nervous because of what Connor had said: the calm before the storm. Watches were one and a half hours each for a twenty-four-hour ride to get to Georges Bank 180 nautical miles east-southeast of Nantucket Island (1 nautical mile = 1.1508 statute miles). The boat only did six to eight knots (1 knot = 1.15 miles per hour). I had to wake up Connor for watch on the ride out to sea. That made me really happy because I hated the Buster.

There was a drawer full of candy, candy, and more candy. I loved it all, and I could eat too! The candy made my watch go by much faster, and I was very alert looking for other boats so there were no boat collisions. We had two or three rounds of watches and then, finally, doomsday! The first day was a twenty-hour day, and I remember being so thirsty. At least I wasn't seasick anymore. I got screamed at like a dog that pissed all over the brand-new couch and carpet!

My name was not *Kyle* anymore; it was *sand nigger*. Not quite sure, but I think it was the second or third day, and nobody would give me any water! I remember being so thirsty, all I wanted was some water!

I remember Joe telling me, "If you can find something to put water in, I'll get you some."

I frantically looked around, and in front of me was an empty one-gallon water jug. It was on the bottom of at least seventy-five bait bags, covered in bait slime. The cap wasn't even on the water jug anymore.

I frantically dug into the pile of bags, grabbed the gallon plastic-bottle jug, and whipped it at Joe where he was standing at the wheelhouse door.

Joe grabbed the jug and laughed out loud. "Look at this. It's nasty." And he threw it back at me. Joe said, "If you keep up with the bags, next trawl, I'll give you some water."

I guess that was my full-time job: baiting, banding lobsters, and being a whipping post. Once in a while, I would stack. I really didn't care for stacking one hundred traps five high or die and puking from work exhaustion. For some reason, I couldn't keep up with the bags and banding lobsters at the same time. I was so frustrated, finally, I snapped. And the more I snapped, the more they laughed at me. I was just amusement for them.

We caught a huge lobster (at least twenty to twenty-five pounds). Ron was all excited. He came out on deck with a can of soda, which I thought was for me.

Ron had different plans. He put the can of soda in the crusher claw of the lobster. The lobster crushed the can like nothing, and soda squirted everywhere while Ron tugged on the can, spraying it everywhere. When he went back into the wheelhouse, I grabbed what was left of the can to get a few drops of soda in my mouth. They were laughing their asses off at me as I was trying to get one more drop of soda out of the can.

I remember the sun going down and thinking really bad thoughts. There was a deck hose (a hose that was fed straight seawater from a pump in the engine room, which was a steady blast of salt water out of a two-inch hose). I grabbed the deck hose, and then when nobody was looking, I drank five or six large mouthfuls. When I finally dropped the hose and took my first breath, all I could taste was this strong taste of salt.

Then as fast as I drank the seawater, it came back up—this time, with a sharp acute pain in my gut. I felt even worse when I was seasick, but this time, I didn't want to die. I literally wanted them to die! I curled up into a ball, and I puked up this thick yellow phlegm that came out of my gut. I had a pain in my stomach like somebody stabbed me right in my belly.

We had a short ride to the next trawl, and all three of them went inside the wheelhouse. When the assholes came back out on deck, the Buster screamed at me, "Puke on your own time, sand nigger! And finish baiting your bait bags!"

I felt so weak, I did not even have the strength to argue. I baited the bags and finished the twenty-hour day without water. I thought I'd never have thoughts of killing somebody, but I did at that time. I wanted them all dead!

After I went inside the wheelhouse for dinner, I drank the most milk I've ever had in one sitting. Ron was excited. I broke the record for drinking the most glasses of milk in boat history.

The Buster asked me, "Thirsty, sand nigger?"

They all had one more laugh before I turned in for the night.

I remember I went right to my rack. Joe asked me something, and I pretended to be asleep. I remember tears just kept streaming from my eyes, and there was no expression on my face. I was just staring at the hull (the side of the boat).

The next day was the last day. Everybody was in a good mood except me. It was to be a day of hauling, and then we were headed home. Everyone was joking with me, trying to get me to laugh. They were asking me over and over, "Are you coming back?" By the end of the night, I felt like somewhat part of the crew, and it put a little smile on my face again. The next day, we always cleaned and scrubbed the boat.

As for the Buster, the only time he was ever happy was when the boat was heading home. He would say, "We're going home, sand nigger. We're going home." And he would rub his big hand on my head!

I liked scrubbing the boat with Connor; he was funny. "Time to brush the boat's teeth, Kyle."

Then he told me, after I learned a few things, I would make half share then full share. Connor said he made one thousand dollars this trip for five days and only worked three days.

I did not believe him, and he said, "Go ask Ron. He'll tell you."

Of course, I didn't ask. I felt betrayed by Ron. How could a man be so nice to someone then be so mean to someone? I was bewildered.

When we arrived at the dock, everybody acted like nothing happened. I went with it too. I wanted that thousand-dollar paycheck. I didn't tell anybody what happened. Just God and I knew what had happened!

I got my first paycheck. Ron always and still does hold a week behind $325. Seemed a lot better working three days. It validated me that I made just as much money as my father, who was a schoolteacher.

Ron looked at me like I had three heads when I said I would go again. I didn't think he expected me to. Ron still didn't mention or apologize to me for what had happened, and I don't think he had any intention to either.

The Buster came over to me with a smile. He asked, "You want a ride home, sand nigger? Your seabag's already in the truck. Let's go." At least he was smiling.

I thought it was kind of an apology from the guys when they put my seabag in the truck for me.

When I got to Exit 6 in Plymouth, I hopped out of the truck and grabbed my seabag. As I started walking toward the exit ramp, I could feel my whole body abruptly move from the vehicles whizzing by me.

I was raised not to be a quitter. Everybody was bragging about how hard the job was. They were so proud of me at eighteen years old. The average age at the time on the deck was thirty-five years old—that's when a man is going through his prime. I was actually scared for the first time in my whole life!

*****

When I was home, I started eating supper at 11:00 p.m. That's when we ate dinner on the boat. Sometimes we ate dinner for breakfast from working till you could see the crest of the sun rise. That was Ron's favorite meal: dinner for breakfast.

My mom walked by me while I was eating dinner and asked, "Is this when you eat dinner on the boat?"

I said yes.

She replied, "Are you kidding me?"

I changed the subject really quickly.

I really love my mom! When I was younger, it hurt me just to think about doing or saying something to hurt my mom's feelings. She was a very quiet, soft-spoken, and very easygoing soul. She's the best mom anyone could ever have! My stepmom told my biological mother she deserved a Purple Heart for putting up with my father. My stepmom ended up in a psych ward.

My biological mom always told me, "Kyle, you are going to be somebody special one day!"

Ron called me the day before we were supposed to go fishing and asked if I was still going. I told him yes. And my tone had changed, like when you really hurt somebody's feelings, how you treat them differently.

Ron said, "Great. I'll be picking you up at Exit 6 the usual time."

I was really beginning to dislike this man!

I dreaded packing my seabag. I wanted to tell my mom so badly what had happened, but I couldn't. When I got to the boat, I didn't even ask what to do. I grabbed my one hundred bait bags and started baiting. I felt different inside, like a ball of rage was building. I was starting to feel mean inside when I knew I had a kind heart.

We had left the dock early, and I had most of the bait bags done. I didn't talk to anyone or even look anyone in the eye for that matter. Everybody was inside, and I finished up the one hundred bait bags.

The wheelhouse door opened, and Joe came out with a hot dog. Joe asked if I wanted anything on my hot dog. I said no. I remember feeling a lot of anger and rage to the point that my eyes started to water. I could not stop my eyes from watering, no matter how hard I tried.

Joe looked at me, laughing a little. "What are you crying for?"

I said I didn't know.

He told me, "Men do not cry or eat quiche."

I do not think he told anybody because I'm sure they would have given me all kinds of grief over it.

*****

It was the end of March—the beginning of April anyways. The weather was getting a little better, but the water temperature was still 42 degrees at Georges Bank.

Ron said there was some bad weather coming. We had better get right to our racks and get some sleep. Then he laughed out loud. Ron was not kidding either.

We worked three days straight with no sleep. I remember Connor, Joe, and Buster singing "Sunrise, Sunset" over and over and over. As soon as the sun came up, you would get your second wind. It reminded me of the movie my dad took me to see *Fiddler on the Roof.*

I said to myself, "Well, at least nothing bad happened to me this trip." (Or so I thought.)

The third day was over, and they decided to clean the boat after a round of watches for a little rest.

I washed up and went to my rack. The next thing I knew, the Buster held me down, and Connor had a stick of butter. Connor pulled my pants down and tried to jam a stick of butter in my ass! I was screaming to the point where Ron finally said, "Come on, guys. Cut it out."

Connor looked at the stick of butter and said, "You got hair in my butter." And he really tried to jam the butter really hard like he meant it!

Then the Buster threw me so hard, my head hit the starboard side hull, and I saw a white flash. I was so tired.

Then the next day, just like clockwork, everyone was in a good mood because we were going home.

I was all done. No more. I did not care anymore. I was so humiliated. How could I ever tell anybody what happened? There was no way! It took me thirty years just to put it on paper!

I had money from my previous check, so I took the bus home. When I left the boat, I did not say anything to anybody. I just left or kind of snuck out, more or less. I did not call Ron. I thought he would figure it out for himself.

Well, I guessed wrong and then some. He called two days later, asking if I needed a ride.

I told him, "I don't think I want to go fishing anymore."

Ron said that he already talked to the guys, that they were going to leave me alone. He said, "Spring is almost here. And you will start learning more, and I will put you on quarter share."

So, of course, like a young fool, I said, "Okay. I will meet you at the bottom of Exit 6."

My heart still did not want to go fishing. I hated Jimmy for getting me this job! Deep down, I knew I wasn't raised to be a quitter. When I arrived home every trip, I would take the bus to the Hanover

Mall and buy myself something. I would buy clothes or a part to my remote-control airplane. The plane was a P-47 with a six-foot wingspan and an eleven-inch propeller, and the gas tank held twelve ounces of fuel with a .06 engine. My brother Antonio helped me put the fuselage and wings together. I also had the most awesome fish tank: a fifty-five-gallon freshwater tank. I remember the angelfish and neon tetras, but I forget the ones I didn't like.

I liked my life! I sit here now and wonder what happened to that good kid!

I went to see a psychiatrist a few years back. He asked me to picture myself as a child playing in my favorite spot. So I asked him how old of a child was I supposed to be.

And he said, "Old enough for you to understand what someone says to you." He continued, "Picture yourself now, at your present age, walking into that spot where you played all the time. What would you say to that little boy?"

I couldn't say anything to the psychiatrist. Tears just started flowing from my eyes with no emotion on my face. In my younger days, I'd call it my tough cry.

I do not believe in that tough stuff anymore. Over the years, I've experienced a lot of things, being out to sea for thirty years. One of them is, the tougher you act, the weaker you are inside. I've seen a lot of men come down the dock acting like Mr. Tough Guy.

Then we would be in twenty- to thirty-foot seas, and Mr. Tough Guy looked out the wheelhouse door with the look of fear in his eyes. Then Mr. Tough Guy was crying, "We're going to die! I'm not going on deck, and you can't make me!"

Some big tough guy actually said that to the captain one day in the Gulf of Maine!

*****

I had one day left before I met Ron on Exit 6. My mom knew something was wrong with me. I couldn't hide it well enough. I told her, "I am okay. I just need a trip off and spend some time home. I'll be okay."

The day came when I had to meet Ron at the bottom of Exit 6 in Plymouth, Massachusetts. I didn't sleep very well that night, and I felt empty inside and all alone.

When he picked me up, he acted like nothing happened, and I was not going to say anything either. I felt like taking the steering wheel and grabbing it really hard to make the truck crash into the woods. I was so angry deep down inside.

When we got to the dock, everybody was already there loading bait. I didn't say a word or look anybody in the eye for that matter. I just put my seabag in the forecastle and then grabbed my one hundred bait bags tied to the rail, and I started to bait the bags.

Joe talked to me like I was seven years old. "Kyleee. Oh, Kylee. Oh, Kyleeeee." For some reason, Joe always put a smirk or maybe a little smile on my face.

Ron said, "We are going to move some lobster gear, so get the tie-downs ready to go. (Tie-downs were seven-fathom pieces of rope a quarter inch thick. They were used to tie down the stacks of lobster traps to move them.)

I started getting faster with the bait bags after they finally told me to grab the redfish by the eyes!

The weather was getting really nice, but it still had a cold bite in the air.

I got some good news from the Buster. The miserable bastard told me he was taking next trip off, and that put a big smile on my face.

I finished my hundred bait bags in record time. Then I ate my hot dog and went right to my rack.

Everybody stayed up, which was unusual considering we would not have much sleep for the next few days. When we got to the gear, it was all business, making one-hundred-trap trawls into fifty-trap trawls. Ron only connected the trawls together in the wintertime.

I was starting to rail, middle, and stack the gear. I still needed to learn twine work and knots. It was the end of the trip, and I knew something usually happened besides being told to look for the line stretcher in the lazaret for over an hour. It was a fool's errand, a task or activity that had no success.

I dropped the bait bucket overboard by accident. Ron had us empty the old bones that were in the bait bag into a bucket. Then when the bucket was full, I would dump the bones overboard.

Ron told me it was blowing fifty knots of winds, and someone emptied a bait bag overboard, and the guy stacking traps downwind got a fish bone in the eyeball making his way back to the next trap. I can't imagine fish poison in your eyeball!

Well, this time, the bucket slipped and went right into the ocean. Ron freaked out. "My bucket! My bucket!"

Joe said, "Go get it."

I said, "Fuck you. The water is forty-two degrees. No way!"

Ron was backing the boat down hard, yelling, "What the fuck! Stupid fucking moron! You make me want to abuse you!"

I thought to myself, *I've seen my brother whipped with dog chain. How much worse can that get?*

I was at the stern, hanging on the stern rail, while Joe was trying to push me into the ocean. I was so angry and fed up, I looked at Joe square in the eyes and said, "You want your fucking bucket?" Then I leaped in the water for the bucket.

I remember hearing this *wow wow wow wow* from the engine or propeller—maybe both. I didn't know, but I did know I couldn't swim that well with my boots filled with water.

Somebody threw me a life ring, and I grabbed it. And the next thing I knew, there was Ron on the stern of the boat with a camera, taking my picture. He said, "This is going make a great picture for my slide show at the end of the year."

His father, Steve Howard, started the survival party. Well, the survival party consisted of, basically (the truth), who could take the most abuse.

I couldn't believe how cold forty-two-degree seawater is until you're actually in it. Ron let me take a shower and change my clothes. I heard Ron yelling at Joe, "Why did you throw him in the water? Kyle could sue me for that."

Joe said to Ron, "Kyle, the crazy bastard, jumped in the water for the bucket."

I put my boots and foul-weather gear in the engine room to dry, and the boat had lots of new boots and foul-weather gear from people before me who had quit and left everything behind.

The day finally ended, and I couldn't wait to get home and get away from everybody. Everyone was real nice, especially the Buster. He was going to Disney World with his kids in Florida. I wish I had a dollar every time he threatened to suck my eye out and fuck my eye socket!

Ron asked if I wanted to bring some lobsters home. I knew he didn't want me to quit, so I took advantage of taking some lobster home with me. The days off went by faster and faster every trip I had off.

When we arrived at the dock to go fishing again, there was another greenhorn who was filling in for the Buster. He was older than I was—early twenties or so. I thought to myself, *Maybe it's his turn, and they will leave me alone for a change.*

I already could see it coming. Joe was already giggling about the next trip, staring at the greenhorn and whispering to the experienced deckhands.

I was so glad to be home and see my mom and even the fish I didn't like in my fish tank for that matter. I lost touch with Jimmy. It seemed like our fishing trips were opposite each other. I was relieved that there was somebody new to maybe take the focus off me. I didn't know how much more I could take.

I did my usual thing at home—cleaned my fish tank and went to the Hanover Mall to see a girl I had a crush on. She worked in one of the stores I frequented. I was supposed to practice my knots and splicing when I got home, but my heart just wasn't into it very much.

The days seemed to go by faster and faster, it seemed, in between trips off. It had been four trips so far, and I had made $1,300 so far. It does not seem like a lot of money, but for me (being eighteen years old at the time), it was a real lot of money. That was back in 1986. Today's calculation in 2020, it would have been equivalent to $3,080.26.

*****

Ron made his usual phone call to find out what time to meet him at Exit 6 in Plymouth. I took the usual ride in the bed of the truck. At least it was the beginning of April and a lot warmer than in February.

When we got to the boat, I did my usual thing. I made my rack then went on deck and started baiting the bait bags. This time, I had a little help from the new guy. I don't even remember his name; he only lasted one trip. Joe said the ratio was just as high as the navy SEALs when it came to who made it here.

I said to him, "I can't imagine why." I did not look at him as I was filling the bait bags.

It was nice to get some help with the bait bags for a change. I made sure to tell the new guy to grab the redfish by the eyes, but I was still watching him get stuck with every redfish he grabbed reluctantly.

I went to the rail to practice my clove hitch knot. There are about seven knots you need to know on deck just to get by, and everyone seemed to leave me alone when I was practicing my knots. It looked like the new guy was on the bottom of the totem pole. I was nice to him, and he was nice to me. I liked that!

We finally got on our way. I filled the new guy in as much as I could about railing, middling, stacking, baiting, and banding. I told him, "You had better eat and go right to your rack to get as much sleep as you can."

He asked why.

"Because we work eighteen-to-twenty-hour days, and sometimes we'll work around the clock for days if bad weather's coming."

He looked at me like I had three heads, and his eyes looked like they were going to pop out of his head!

I was elated this trip that the Buster was not here and there was another greenhorn. *Maybe I'll get quarter share*, I thought to myself.

When we got to the fishing grounds, the weather wasn't very nice out, and the greenhorn was puking everywhere. I wasn't about to tell him to puke on his own time.

Joe was screaming off the top of his lungs at both of us. We did not make enough bait bags, and he couldn't keep up and could barely stand up for that matter. The greenhorn looked like a drunkard who was stumbling all over the place and puking on himself. I didn't look at the wheelhouse window very much at all. When I did, Ron always had a look like he hated you or a stupid "I love it" smirk on his face.

The greenhorn was real thirsty, and they tried that same thing with him, except I had water stashed everywhere in the lazaret, fish-hold, gear locker, and crew locker. The greenhorn couldn't believe I kept coming back to this abuse trip after trip.

Connor was the cook on most of the trips. I liked when Connor cooked. He would always explain to me in detail what we were having for supper.

We had one day to go, and the weather was getting better and better. Weather has a major impact on how fast you get through the gear.

The greenhorn was still queasy. That just meant I got to eat a lot more, and I was growing stronger. I could feel it.

Something told me that the greenhorn was not coming back anytime soon. I liked it when Joe told me stories about other guys that didn't make it. One greenhorn hated the job so bad, after a fishing trip, when they got back to the dock to tie the boat up, he hopped on the dock. He was supposed to catch the dock lines. Instead, he ran to his car and took off, leaving his seabag and everything else he brought with him!

The last day was Joe's scream day. I remember because when we were cleaning the boat, he took a long-handle Sparta scrub brush. (The brushes are supposed to be unbreakable.) Joe whacked the brush on the sorter top, where the lobsters were to be banded, and he broke it. He grabbed another one and said, "I'm going to do that to your head."

So I lunged on top of the sorter table, bowed my head, and said, "Go ahead. I don't fucking care anymore!"

I was waiting for a whack on the head. He laughed and tapped the brush gently on top of my head and walked away laughing.

The new guy saw what happened and couldn't believe what I did. Do you know what? I couldn't believe it either. I think that was when I first started getting a set of balls. I look back now to when I was eighteen years old, and I ask myself what the heck I was thinking going 180 nautical miles offshore!

Believe it or not, I gained some respect from Joe that day. I did the same thing as last time when the boat got to the dock. I took the bus ride home to Plymouth, but this time, I left in better spirits.

When I got home, I ran into Jimmy. He said he might be leaving his spot on the boat, and I could probably take his site if I wanted. He asked me how it was going on the boat, and I told him it was great. I think he knew something went on, but he didn't pry at all to try and get it out of me.

He told me a story when he was on the *Sea Slave*. They found out he was claustrophobic, so they locked him in the lazaret for a long time.

I told him a few minor things that happened. I thought the rest of the other events would go to my grave with me, or so I thought.

*****

Ron called to see if I still wanted to go next trip. I wanted to tell him different. My father always told me to never quit a job unless you had one in your back pocket. He used to say, "Always keep a job in your back pocket too." My father told me, "Once your boss starts casting a shadow over you, it's time to move on." (*Casting a shadow* means when someone is behind you, looking at what you're doing, and the sun is on his back, casting a shadow on the ground in front of you.)

I wasn't sure if I had that other site on Jimmy's boat, so I decided to make another trip. I was changing from that sweet kid into a sour and angry kid. At least I knew it was coming to an end.

I met Ron at Exit 6, and Joe was with him. We actually had a good laugh, believe it or not. Ron's brother-in-law Paul knew the Buster was going to Disney World. So Paul called Ron and said, "I see the Buster went to Disney World." Ron asked Paul how he knew, and Paul replied, "I was watching TV, and a Disney World commercial came on, and Mickey Mouse was wearing an eye patch."

Things seemed a little different, but the damage had been done. Deep down, I hated these people from the pit of my stomach.

When we got to the boat, it was business as usual. I made my rack, grabbed my bait bags, baited them, and stayed out of everybody's way. I tried anyway, seeing as how I was on a sixty-five-foot boat with nowhere to go but in the ocean. I was so not happy about even looking at the Buster. I wouldn't even make eye contact with him at all.

I needed a lot of work on my twining. Twine repair was the mesh on the lobster trap. I kept practicing my knots and splicing (to join or connect a rope or ropes by interweaving the strands). I would try to repair a large hole in the twine of the lobster trap, and Joe would say it looked like a spider's web.

I kept practicing. Deep down, I was determined to learn what I needed to know.

Connor showed up at the boat with another black eye. He loved to drink and start barroom fights—seemed like it anyways. One time, there was a restaurant in the North Shore. Well, it was a ship made into a restaurant with porthole windows at the galley tables. (The boat-shaped restaurant in Lynnfield, Massachusetts, dates back to 1930. It closed in January 2017.) Connor went to leave the restaurant, and this well-dressed, stuck-up man was looking down at Connor like he was better than him, to put it nicely. Well, Connor punched right through the porthole window and hit the guy right in the face. Talk about spoiling your dinner plan!

I don't know why I looked up to all the bar fights and stuff. Maybe I'm trying to figure out where I went wrong in my life.

We finally left the dock. This was to be my last trip with this prick! I cannot believe I even went on that trip. I was so angry with myself, I did not care anymore. They would call me sand nigger, and I would snap at everyone and call them a piece of dung. They all knew they brought me to my snapping point. Joe nicknamed me "Spaz" by the second day. I was losing it at everyone, but little did I know, that's what the men all wanted. I was feeding fuel to the fire a shovelful of coal at a time.

The trip went along okay, or so I thought. We were cleaning the boat, and Connor was the cook, so he cleaned inside the boat. The head (the bathroom) was midship to the stern, and there was a porthole window. Connor poked his head out the window and yelled, "Kyle, come here and look at this."

At first, I said, "Fuck you!" Then he showed me a picture of a beautiful Playboy centerfold, and I was captivated. It also reminded me of a saying my father always said: "You can't make a horse drink water, but you can put salt in his mouth to make him thirsty!"

So I ran over in a flash to get a peek. He said "look," so I stuck my head in the porthole window. Then I heard this hissing sound, and the next thing I felt were my eyes burning like they were on fire. The son of a bitch sprayed Lysol disinfecting spray in my eyes!

I ran, tripped, stumbled, and rolled my way over to the deck hose. I blasted my eyes with the salt water for a long time. I was so mad that I didn't get mad. I still couldn't understand that feeling inside. I felt rage then numbness then nothing. It scared me a little. I grabbed my scrub brush and started scrubbing again, bewildered about what had just happened to me.

When we got to the dock, there was a big green boat called *Anna Bo*. Joe was cursing the boat and the old man that owned the boat. They nicknamed Steve Howard the "old man." He was the owner of the boat. I guess Joe had an old score they never settled. I really didn't give a damn. I was kind of glad this old man pissed Joe off.

The *Anna Bo* was a swordfish and offshore lobster boat owned by Ron Howard's father, Steve Howard.

Joe wanted to give me a tour of the boat. I really didn't care to, but I went anyway (like I really had a choice). She was 110 feet long and big as a house with all the amenities. The wheelhouse was high. It was a double-decker. The wheelhouse was huge. And in the middle of the wheelhouse, there was a set of stairs that brought you downstairs to the entrance of the deck and the entrance to the engine room. From there, to get to the engine room, you had to go down another flight of stairs.

The galley was beautiful. It had a full double-door refrigerator, an oven, a microwave, and a TV/VCR. Across the hall, there was a walk-in refrigerator that was ten by ten feet. It was cube shaped and six feet high with wire racks on either side. It looked like a mini grocery store. The shelves were stuffed with food, and the floor was also packed with food under the wire shelving racks with just enough room to walk in the center to get what you needed.

The captain had his own stateroom in the wheelhouse. There were two staterooms forward of the galley—one on the port and one on the starboard side of the boat. It was two men per room: one upper rack and one lower rack. Then back down the hallway midship, there was another set of stairs going down to the forecastle. In the forecastle, there was room for six men to sleep with all kinds of shelves and drawers. There was even a washer and dryer across from the galley.

Out on deck was unbelievable. The deck was huge. It looked like a tennis court compared to the *Sea Slave*'s deck. The fishhold could hold one hundred thousand pounds of fish, and the lobster tank could hold forty thousand pounds of lobster. The boat even had a saltwater chilling system to keep the salt water in the lobster tank at a temperature of forty-two degrees, just like the supermarkets do. Forty-two degrees is the optimum temperature for lobsters in a holding tank.

The *Anna Bo* impressed me a lot. I was glad I went on that tour; it opened my eyes. I wanted to go swordfishing.

Joe told me, "No you don't."

I told Joe, "Yeah, you just want to keep me for your own little sand-nigger."

He laughed and hit me on the back of the head lightly.

I went on my way to catch the bus home to Plymouth. I couldn't tell Ron that I quit without knowing if I had another job or not yet. I was so angry and full of rage, I didn't even call Ron or answer his phone calls for a ride to the boat. I figured he would get the hint this time.

I went to Jimmy's house the next day that I was supposed to be at the boat to leave. Jimmy had an offer for me to listen to, and his father was there also, just going in and out of the kitchen every so often, catching snippets of our conversation at the kitchen table Jimmy and I were sitting at.

"Jimmy," I said with a serious tone in my voice while looking him straight in the eyes. I told him I had enough of the *Sea Slave*, and I needed a break.

Jimmy laughed. He said, "I don't blame you one bit." And he said, "Listen. I'm thinking of selling my motorcycle and going to Florida."

It was music to my ears—an out!

Jimmy's father walked in the kitchen and said, "Nick is looking for Kyle. He wants his body for the next fishing trip."

His son chimed in. "This is none of your business!"

I said, "I want to know your opinion."

His father replied, "I think you should go fishing."

I finally made up my mind what I was going to do! I decided to go to Florida with Jimmy.

I remember that day when I made that decision at Jimmy's house. It feels like it was yesterday! My uncle Fred was selling his house in Daytona Beach, Florida. I was going to help him pack up his belongings and try to find a job. When we got there, he welcomed us to stay, but he did not like the idea of me staying in Florida.

I got up very early every morning to look for a job except on Sundays. Sunday was the only day we did not have chores in the house growing up, and it stuck with me.

Jimmy hated Florida, and when we finished helping pack up my uncle Fred's belongings, Jimmy drove back to Massachusetts with Fred. Uncle Fred's next-door neighbor let me stay there until I could find a job.

Every Sunday, I would go to this hotel and swim and lie in the sun. One Sunday, this lifeguard came up to me. She asked if I could tell people I used this suntan lotion, and she would let me have some. I said okay. It was very expensive. It was $20 for 8 oz. That Sunday, she sold a lot of suntan lotion. So the next Sunday, I came back to the hotel again, but this time, there was somebody there to meet me.

This man came over to me with the lifeguard. He explained who he was and that he owned Sun Sation Beach & Ski Club. The owner Rick Harrison even had a house for the employees to stay at rent-free. It seemed too good to be true at first, but when I saw the Porsche he took me for a ride in to the main office, I was sold.

He told me that I would not be a lifeguard, and I would be selling suntan lotion. "There will be a lifeguard on duty, so it will not interfere with your selling," he said.

The people that lived in the house where he put me up were older than me. They were all college students working for the summer, trying to pay their way through college.

They taught me how to sell suntan lotion. I thought it was going to be kind of easy at first. You needed a sales pitch, and then you needed a closing. The trick was that whoever talked first at the closing, lost—meaning, after you make your closing, be quiet. Don't say anything. Just wait. About 90 percent of the time, people will get uncomfortable and say yes, or they want to get rid of you and tan. Another good sales pitch they taught me was to get the person to say yes a lot. When you ask them to buy it, they'll say yes because you've trained them to say yes many times already. You just had to think of questions to ask that would make them say yes.

The first week, I did excellent, and every week after, I excelled more and more. A few months passed, and Rick asked me if I wanted to go to Las Vegas. I was to sell suntan lotion for the company out there. Of course, I said yes in a heartbeat. There were only two people going out of twenty: Julia and me.

We arrived at Las Vegas in the daytime. He had somebody was waiting at the gate for us to take us to the Aladdin Hotel. It wasn't open for gambling yet; it was in the process of new ownership.

A Japanese man, Ginji Yasuda, bought it for fifty-four million and invested millions more to upgrade the hotel. Ginji Yasuda was the flamboyant international playboy who was the first foreigner ever to be granted a Nevada gambling license when he took over the troubled Aladdin Hotel.

The first night I was there, I noticed a corvette out front of the hotel. Police were everywhere with yellow ribbon all around the vehicle. The next day, the area manager of Sun Solutions told us the man blew his brains out with a gun because he lost all his money.

The area manager divided Julia and me up. He took me to the Dunes Hotel. The hotel was beautiful; they had two huge pools. It was early in the morning, about 6:00 a.m. or so. The district manager, Todd, looked at me and said, "Well, go sell some lotion!"

There was a salesman at the desk reading the newspaper. I looked around and saw only one or two people. So I walked over to a couple sitting near the booth and made my first sale. I sold them the whole suntan lotion kit. I still remember the kit: Aloe Mink ($20), Sun Dazzler ($10), Tan Accelerator ($9), After-Sun Lotion ($13.50), and Aloe Gel—the large bottle was $15 and the small bottle was $7.50. Then I sold SPF 8 and SPF 4 for $8 each.

Todd took the room charge slip and slapped it in front of the kid on the sign-in desk. Then he took me to the Las Vegas Hilton. I couldn't believe my eyes. The pool deck was on the third floor above ground. At that time, it was the biggest hotel in the world. It seemed like there were countless lounge chairs all around the pool. There were valets to carry a cushion pad and towel to your chair.

First, you had to sign in with the pool manager, Gary. Then he sold you some suntan oil, raft rental, or sunglasses. Then the pool boy would follow the guest to the chair. He would put the pad on the chair, then the towel on the arm of the chair, and they would give him a tip.

I remember the area manager asking me, "Why are you here, Kyle?"

I said, looking at the pool deck in awe, "People bring money here, and I'm here to take it away."

He took his sunglasses off, smiled, and asked me how old I was.

Poor Julia. Rick, the owner of Sun Sation, told me when Julia stepped out on deck, she went in shock because it was so big, and there were so many more people than in Florida's pool decks. Rick sent Julia back to the Aladdin Hotel. He wanted to bring me to the Hilton to see what would happen to me. I guess I passed the test. Then he sent me back to the Aladdin Hotel to talk to Julia.

When I got to the hotel, Julia was not there. I called Rick and told him, "I will work with Julia for a couple of days at the Las Vegas Hilton."

Todd, the area manager, picked us up in the morning and took us to the Tropicana Apartments, where we were going to stay. It was beautiful. There was a pool, weight room, sauna, and whirlpool. He gave us some money and told us to get adjusted. He said, "Go get some food or eat out or whatever." He was very curt.

There were already new pots and pans, and even the glasses and silverware were new. The location was great; it was a walking distance to the supermarket. They called the convenience stores Stop & Go. They were everywhere.

Nevada is a very tough state on drugs. If you got caught with one joint, it was mandatory jail time in 1986, and you needed a sheriff's card to get a job anywhere. On the back of the sheriff's card, it said, "$1,000 reward for any information about drugs or crime!" It seemed like the town of Las Vegas was breeding rats.

All I kept hearing were stories about people killing themselves over losing money. One lady jumped off the top of a hotel; she had lost her life savings. I could not understand gambling. I was always taught by my father that one seed in my hand was worth a whole crop.

The day came when I was trying to help Julia try to sell. I ended up selling enough to keep us both afloat. The area manager, Todd, ended up finding out about me selling for her and flew her back to Florida the same day.

One thing I learned in Las Vegas was that stars were no more like any one of us. I was on the pool deck of the Las Vegas Hilton, and way in the back part of the pool was Morgan Fairchild and her boyfriend, and a couple of bodyguards were with her. I asked if she wanted some sunblock, and I offered her the SPF 25 because she was literally glowing white. Her boyfriend was wearing a Speedo bikini underwear that said Playboy on the front with silver glitter on the lettering. He wasn't even in good shape, in my eyes.

Morgan Fairchild wanted some oil, so I told her mink oil was the closest oil to the human skin.

Her boyfriend said, "Is my dog going to start humping my leg when I get home?"

She replied, "I don't know these people."

That's when I realized my dad was right; every person has to put his or her pants on one leg at a time.

They finished the Aladdin Hotel, and I was offered the job as pool manager. The hotel manager at the time was Mr. Paladeno. He liked me. I took the bull by the horns, he said.

I filled out all kinds of requisitions to order things I needed for the pool. I figured if he spent fifty-four million, what's a couple thousand to him?

The pool was beautiful. It was hand-laid Italian tile with awesome designs in it.

I got to know this security guard very well. He would tell me stories and make me laugh.

My favorite story was this lady who thought she was locked in her room. She kept trying to open the door frantically to the point where she was rubbing the flesh off her hand. She finally called security, screaming and panicking. When they got to the room, they realized she was trying to open the door that was attached to the other room next to hers! He said she had sleep deprivation from being up so many days. Having fun gambling and drinking causes you not to think right.

Then there was the story of poor Ginji Yasuda's poodle. I felt bad for the dog; it wasn't funny. One security guard's job was to play ball with the dog every morning. Ginji Yasuda, the owner, lived on the top floor of the hotel. Well, one security guard was supposed to watch the dog. While he was playing ball, he accidently threw the ball too far, and the ball went off the roof. The dog ran after the ball and fell to its death.

One day I will never forget. He came to the pool deck all shook up, shaking nervously like he had seen a ghost. So I asked the security guard what had happened. He did not want to tell me at first. Then I promised him I would never tell a soul. I told him the first thing I was taught on the boat was that whatever was said on this boat stays on this boat! I think he needed to tell someone to get it off his chest, like a confession in church. I think that's why people eventually get themselves caught. The guilt is so unbearable for their mind and soul, they get caught so they can put their tattered consciences to rest and finally move on with their lives!

A man lost his life savings and took a sawed-off shotgun to his room and blew half his head off! Then they made a couple of Aladdin Hotel security guards clean up the mess. Unfortunately, he was one of them.

I couldn't fathom why someone would do that. I actually tried to imagine the scenario in my head, and I couldn't imagine it. For the first time in my whole life, I finally started to think about what life was all about. It changed my way of thinking—the way I was living my life that day!

You would not hear about these acts in the paper or on TV. The town kept it very quiet.

I started to dislike Las Vegas. I figured Las Vegas out, why everything was so cheap: drinks and food. They lowered the value of living so you would lose your value for the dollar. At least it seemed that way.

I remember at the Horseshoe Hotel (a smaller but popular place), it had a big horseshoe. It was so big, you could walk through it. The face of it was all glass with a million dollars placed in it ever so neatly stacked. You could actually see what a million dollars looked like! It was an amazing aura, standing under a million dollars and looking at all that money!

After midnight, you could get a big sirloin steak and eggs with all the fixings for $1.99. You just might have to put up with an inebriated old-timer taking a fork, putting an open soft-package pat of butter on it, then taking his finger and putting it on the tip of the fork. Firmly holding on to the handle of the fork with his other hand, he then pulled his finger that was on the tip of the fork as hard as he could and take aim at the guy sitting a couple patrons next to you. Finally, he let go of his fingertip and got a perfect shot on my cheek so hard that it actually stuck to my face!

I actually didn't even get mad at the drunk man. I was actually impressed with his shot. I couldn't believe how good of a shot the man was for how drunk he was! I felt bad for the man, and I wasn't twenty-one years old to be able to bicker about it either.

I really missed Shane, the only close friend I made in Nevada. I'm glad I made his acquaintance. If it wasn't for Shane showing me the ropes on how things worked out there, I wouldn't have lasted as long as I did! I truly missed Shane. One day, I will find my friend again to laugh at all the pranks and stunts he pulled on all the newcomers to Las Vegas! And believe me, he did a really good job at almost making you piss your pants—literally! How? you ask. Well, at the Las Vegas airport (way in the back of the airport), there is a dip near the chain-link fence. Shane loved to take his first-timers to that spot (who had never been to Vegas before) to smoke his *indica* (California mountain-grown marijuana). After you took a couple of puffs and you were tripping from the high potency of the THC, Shane would sit back and watch the show start. He would sit back in the driver's seat of his souped-up Trans Am with T-tops that were off just so the sadistic bastard could view the full effects as his new friend wigged the fuck out. I'm not sure a lot of people would have sat there, calm as a cucumber, seeing a huge commercial airline jet's landing gear fully deployed then get the feeling of the suction from the plane flying over your head. It felt like the car lifted off then slammed back on the ground again! You know what? The car probably did, all while you were seeing your life flash before your eyes!

My friend Shane was with me the night there was an assault and battery with a pat of butter at the Horseshoe Casino Hotel! Shane was the one that made a big stink about what the drunk man did, but before I could even excuse and forgive the man, the Horseshoe Hotel security guards already started escorting him out of the hotel.

One day, I was working with a salesman. The tan man called himself Andy. He was at the Aladdin Hotel to help me sell suntan lotion that day.

While we were on the pool deck selling, I heard him say, "I'm thirty-nine years old. Look at my skin. I've been in the sun my whole life, and look how good it still looks."

Then I heard some guy in the background nearby say, "Yeah, thirty-nine and declining."

That's when I realized I did not want to do this for the rest of my life!

When I got home, there was a yellow piece of paper on the doorknob. It was a Western Union note from my father. It said, "Please call me when I got home. Love, Dad." I couldn't believe he found me three thousand miles away from home. I was bewildered.

The next day, I called my father at home. He told me his long-time friend Mr. Burgis was dying of cancer. Mr. Burgis lived on Mashpee Lake on Cape Cod, Massachusetts. I have a lot of great memories staying there when I was growing up in the summertime. He was just as much a friend to me as to my father also. I really loved this man.

Mr. Burgis was 100 percent Wampanoag Indian. He taught me my first fishing knot. He told me a story about this huge tanker ship far offshore that will last in my memory for a lifetime. He said these colossal tanker ships would run over fishing gear, and when it went under the boat, the propeller would chew the fishing gear up and spit them out! He was talking about lobster gear—the ball and high flyers. When you got the high flyer and ball back from hauling the other end first, the high flyer pole was in a complete circle, and the ball was flattened by the huge propeller, which was twenty-two feet wide and weighed forty-three tons. Today's cost of a tanker ship propeller is close to half a million dollars. Hence, that's why you have two ends—in case one end sinks from the high seas or is run over by one of these supertanker ships Mr. Burgis was talking about.

Deep down in the pit my stomach, I missed my family and the ocean severely. It was getting close to fall, and the season was just about to end for selling suntan lotion, and the season for lobstering was just about to start. So I packed up all my belongings, got on a plane, and flew to Boston Logan Airport.

Then right from Logan Airport, my father asked me, "Do you want to go home and get some rest or keep traveling north to see Mr. Burgis?"

Of course, I said travel north.

From Boston, we drove straight to White River Junction in Vermont. That's where Mr. Burgis retired. He was a chemistry teacher at the same high school my father taught at on Cape Cod. It was a hell of a long trip nonstop to get there from Las Vegas, I'll tell you that much.

When I got to Vermont, I knew Las Vegas was not for me. Leaving the city to just hear birds and crystal clear streams, Vegas was like another world to me. Deep down in my gut, I hated that fast pace of the fake oasis in the desert.

My father and I stayed for a few days then headed back to Cape Cod, Massachusetts. Mr. Burgis wanted to be buried in Mashpee in Cape Cod to have a traditional Wampanoag Indian burial. It was held outside in a beautiful open field surrounded by pine trees, and everybody gathered in a big circle, holding hands.

I remember the speaker at the funeral saying, "If you wish to say something to remember him by, speak out or you may keep it to yourself."

I remember one Indian woman said, "Every winter, when there is a pine tree covered in snow, I will shake the snow off one of the branches to remember you by."

To myself, I said, "Every time I tie the first fishing knot Mr. Burgis taught me when I was a very young troubled boy, and he knew it, I will remember him."

Till this day, every time I tie that fishing knot on my hook, I always remember Mr. Burgis!

I was really glad I had come home. I knew it was here in New England. This was where I belonged—near the ocean.

I went to Plymouth, America's hometown, to see my mom. She told me to call Jimmy as soon as she heard from me again. So I called Jimmy and told him all about my short journey to Las Vegas, Nevada. Jimmy asked if I wanted a real man's job. I said, "Sure but not with Ron Howard."

Jimmy laughed his ass off! He was on his father's boat, named the *Adventure*. It was a seventy-seven-foot new offshore lobster boat. He was getting married and did not want to go offshore fishing anymore.

I jumped all over the fishing site. He even gave me his new foul-weather gear to use.

Mike Bradshaw was the fill-in captain and part owner of the *Adventure*. The boat was seventy-seven feet long, twenty-two feet wide, and had a full galley, head, fridge, stove, microwave, and TV/VCR.

It was almost the end of the year, and I was ready to start a new one. I was still in decent shape. I worked out every night in Nevada and jogged two to three miles a day.

Rick was the full-time captain. He was nicknamed Dead Low Ricky because he always brought the boat home at low tide all the time. Plymouth Harbor has a twelve-foot tide at the dock, so I could see how he got his nickname. Mike was a relief captain and part owner of the boat with Jimmy's father. I had not met the whole crew yet, but Jimmy said they were good guys.

I found a room to rent right down the street from where they kept the boat docked. It was great. The boat ported out of Plymouth (where I was born), and I lived right down the street, a mere walking distance to the boat.

I had made a new acquaintance, Paul Mahoney. He happened to have an extra room to rent and needed the money to make ends meet.

My first trip was great. It was really cold compared to Nevada but much easier than the *Sea Slave*. I still remember the whole crew today like it was yesterday. We had the same crew all winter.

While I was at home, I practiced tying my knots. I'd put the back of the chair on the floor, and then I would practice my knots on one of the legs of the chair until my hands literally bled.

Noah—one of the deckhands on the *Adventure*—understood what I went through on the *Sea Slave*. I liked Noah. He was very patient and taught me a lot of seamanship I didn't know. Noah knew all about the *Sea Slave* and how Ron ran that boat. He said the captain and crew would keep you stupid by not teaching you a damn thing. Then they would abuse you to make you quit so their shares would stay higher. Noah said the ones that stayed on that boat were the few, the proud, and the stupid. Noah said that boat was nicknamed the *Sea Slave*!

I was thinking to myself, *Good thing I left that boat!*

My father always said, "I didn't raise any dummies." And he would hold his fist in the air.

When we got back to the dock, the captain asked if I wanted to go have a beer at the 1620 Restaurant. I wasn't old enough to drink, I told him. He said, "Well, you sure look like you're old enough. Come on!"

We went to the 1620 Restaurant and had a blast. They treated us extra special. Everybody bought rounds of beer for the whole crew, and I had the time of my life!

The year wasn't even over, and Rick (the captain) was fired over a dispute he was having with the boat owner, and they hired a new captain.

The new captain and I didn't get along at all. You've heard of love at first sight? Well, this was hate at first sight. There was something right off the start when we first met each other. I disliked him, and he disliked me.

We were in harvest moon. The lobster run before Thanksgiving is known for a big catch of lobsters, and it's also known for treacherous seas and high winds that can last for days! They're called nor'easters, and I've had three avid captains tell me the same thing: November is the most turbulent month.

Like my father said, "Five people call you a horse, start looking for a saddle."

I guess I still needed the validation of two more captains because...well, that winter, I went out to sea on the *Adventure*. It was the coldest winter in New England in one hundred years. I actually have a picture of me that my friend Paul Mahoney took of me on the deck of the *Adventure*, and behind me in the picture, the whole harbor is frozen over.

November is a bad month of the year for fishermen. The world is changing from fall to winter, and weather patterns get a lot worse with strong storms. And basically, you get the crap beat out of you on deck! The adrenaline high I felt working while riding those twenty-five-to-thirty-foot seas surpasses any high I've ever had—man-made or grown from the earth!

It was November 1987, one week before Thanksgiving. The new Captain Crunch was hard up on crew to make a full trip before Thanksgiving. I asked if I could bring my older brother fishing. He had worked on a lobster boat in Sandwich, Cape Cod, for a few years and became a deck boss. So I called my brother and asked if he wanted to go fishing. He was grateful to have that extra money before Christmas. My brother's real trade was carpentry, and I knew work was slow for him at the moment.

Well, the last trip my brother made with me, I'll never forget. I was cutting a fish for bait and putting it back in the trap. I slipped and cut my knuckle tip off my forefinger right off my hand. The captain stitched me up, and I could actually hear him swallow from the looks of my hand. I couldn't rail, middle, or bait for that matter. So I stacked the rest of the trip—eight hundred traps. I looked at it like it was better than stacking the full set of gear the boat was allotted, which was 1,600 lobster traps at the time.

Well, this trip on the adventure offshore lobster with my brother was even worse! There was really bad weather coming, and all the other boats were heading home except us! The wind came on slow and steady to a whopping 75 to 85 mph. This greedy moron stayed until we literally had to cut the line we were hauling. Then we set the rest of the traps out by pushing them out the open stern. The wind got worse, and at one point, the wind reached 85 to 95 mph, with gusts to 100 miles an hour with seas fifty to sixty feet. Since the wind was out of the northwest, it was really difficult to go home as that was the direction we had to go.

We could only make two and a half knots; that's not very fast. This tanker ship passed us just about dusk, and the captain of the tanker ship called us to see how fast we were going. He said it seemed too fast, and he was worried about our speed. The captain of the tanker ship said they were traveling at five knots, and we should slow it down some.

So what does Captain Crunch do? He hits the throttle a little bit more.

I was well aware of my instincts by then, so I told my brother Antonio, "Let's go down below."

Forward of the galley was a stateroom, where I slept. I had the stateroom with a door. It was nice to have that little bit of solitude. Forward of my stateroom was the forecastle, which was basically the bow (the very front of boat). It had four racks: two on each side of the boat, a top rack, and a bottom rack.

About an hour later, I was staring at the trim above the doorway. I think it was teak or mahogany. Anyways, I heard this indescribable noise—a glass-shattering explosion! At the same time, the piece of wood trim on the top part of the doorway split all the way down the center. The wave that hit the boat actually stalled the (3408) Caterpillar diesel engine from the impact of the wave hitting the boat and flattened the starboard side wave break! (A wave break is a steel flange welded to the bow in front of the wheelhouse windows. It is shaped to deflect the seawater up and over from the bulletproof windows.)

Like I said, you can't compress a liquid. The cleanest cut you can make with steel is water. Sixty thousand pounds per square inch of compressed water shoots through a pinhole and actually makes the cleanest cut you can possibly get on steel. This was a long time ago, and I'm sure there are a few steel cutters laughing at the new technology they have now to cut steel with.

When I quickly opened my stateroom door, to my surprise, all I could see was water coming down the galley stairs. You couldn't even see the stairs. There was so much water, it looked like a waterfall coming into the galley floor.

I quickly shut my door and grabbed my seabag off the floor to put it in my rack so it would stay dry. When I opened the door again, water gushed into my stateroom, and there was three to four feet of seawater in the galley and forecastle and in my stateroom.

Then I saw seabags floating by my stateroom door. As I looked in the forecastle, my brother probably had the same expression I had on my face, with eyes and mouth wide open. I knew the water had to go somewhere, and I was right. It ran all over the ninety-kilowatt Caterpillar diesel generator.

Antonio yelled to me, "Don't go in the water. You'll get electrocuted."

After the breakers blew, I knew it was safe to get in the water. That was when the emergency lights came on.

Antonio and I waded our way to the wheelhouse. We couldn't open the hatch to the galley floor to pump the seawater out because there was a case of lobster bands left on the floor of the wheelhouse. The pressure from the seawater blew open the whole box and even the several one-pound plastic bags the bands were in. One case of lobster bands will band five thousand pounds of lobster at a three-pound average, so you can imagine how many bands there were floating around in the galley. The rubber bands would have clogged the pipe that sucked the seawater out if we had opened the galley hatch.

When I made my way up to the wheelhouse, I couldn't believe my eyes. There were three starboard windows blown out, and the back wheelhouse window was blown as well. All the electronics were on the deck: radar, loran, sounder, and radio. The scary part was the shipyard had special glass put in traditional laminated glass (bulletproof glass). You can't compress a liquid, and this is an excellent example of how much power you can produce with hydraulics! (Hydraulics is the branch of science and technology concerned with the conveyance of liquids through pipes and channels, especially as a source of mechanical force or control.) The compression from the seawater embedded the laminated glass so deep into the woodwork, I couldn't pull it out with a pair of pliers.

I remember Captain Crunch coming out of the engine room. He almost ran over me to get outside, and his hands were shaking like the leaves on a tree. The electrical fire was burning so badly that the engine-room door was glowing like the Sunkist orange. He had a flare gun in his hand and was trying to load it with a flare cartridge. He was shaking so badly, he kept dropping the flare shells. Then when the captain got the flare in the gun, he stepped outside the wheelhouse and pulled the trigger, but the flare didn't go off.

Antonio saw that he opened the cartridge and dropped it right in front of me. Antonio grabbed me and told me to stay away from that shell. They call it slow flash. You're supposed to wait three seconds just in case there is a slow flash in the shell.

The first one and the second one were duds. Then when Captain Crunch shot the third flare, the wind hit the flare like it was a badminton ball—right into the water. The fourth flare he shot with the wind, and it looked like it was a mile away from us in the other direction.

Cyril, the Frenchman, called for me in the galley, so I went to see what he wanted. He screamed out to me to get a five-gallon bucket, so I did. When I got back with the bucket, he had a big salad bowl to fill the bucket up with salt water.

He told me in a deep French accent, "Doon't woory. I've beeen thruu thiss beeforree. It-it'sss nnoothing too wwoory about it."

I loved his accent; it was so cool. I used to make him talk just to hear his accent.

Cyril was so calm in the midst of all the chaos. He told me a story earlier that year about a worse situation. There was a man who broke the world record sailing in a huge catamaran from France to Florida. He decided to do the same thing and try to beat his record. They got caught in a storm, and the catamaran flipped. One man died, one man broke his pelvic bone from landing so hard, and Cyril came out unscathed. After the storm, the catamaran was upside down, drifting with no power to sail anywhere! They put a big black SOS on the hull and drifted for three days. They dove into a shark-infested ocean to get food and had fresh water to drink inside the catamaran before they were (luckily) saved in this vast open ocean!

The French are crazy! They would sail in a bathtub to get anywhere if they had to! I have a lot of respect for the French!

I remember frantically trying to get up the galley stairs to the wheelhouse door to empty the five-gallon bucket of seawater and lobster bands on deck! Then when I frantically went back down to the galley, it turned into total calmness. The next time I came up to the wheelhouse, I remember my brother Antonio putting his survival suit on.

I stopped and asked Antonio, "What are you doing?"

Antonio looked at me square in the eyes, and he said, "If I see the captain putting his survival suit on, I'm damn well sure putting my survival suit on too!"

I could hear Cyril screaming in a deep French accent, "C'est la merde! Kyle! Hurrey up with the bucket!"

C'est la merde means "Shit! This is a disaster!" in French. I love their language. You can swear the nastiest words you can ever imagine, and it all sounds so beautiful to the ears.

Cyril and I finished emptying the whole galley, close to four feet of seawater. My arms were so tired, I could barely lift them anymore. Carrying numerous buckets of water wiped me out, so I ate, got some dry clothes on, and told everybody, "I'm going to my rack. Wake me up when it's over."

Those were my exact words.

The next day, the weather was still nasty. Captain Crunch was in the engine room, still looking for his chest of gold.

Antonio thought of an idea to block the windows. The deck plates in the engine room were diamond-plate aluminum. So Antonio got a jigsaw and cut three square pieces at a size a little bigger than the windows. Then he drilled four holes, one on each corner of the diamond plates. Then he took twelve bottom wood sills, four for each window. (A bottom sill is used on the bottom of each end of lobster trap for the corner post that fit in the holes of the top sills.) On the bottom sill, there was a hole on each end of it that would be perfect for his plan to fix them.

The boat went fair wind, so someone could go outside on the bow of the boat to help patch the windows. Then Antonio took the sills and put two on the outside of the boat (one on top and one on the bottom) and then put two on the inside of the boat the same way as outside the boat. The diamond-plate square was in the middle but outside of the boat. Then he took the banding tool and went through the holes with the stainless band and tightened it up. (A banding tool is a tool used to wrap a stainless steel band to secure the steel weights to the bottom of the high flyers.)

The vessel had power and steering, but we didn't have a compass or loran for navigating, and GPS (global positioning system) wasn't fully operational yet in 1987.

The tanker ship saw our flare and came back to assist us. The aura felt like something out of the movies. Twenty-five yards away from us was a one-thousand-foot tanker ship, and all I could see was a wall of water flowing off the deck. It looked like Niagara Falls—literally enough water to instantly flood our boat to sink us. Not that they could do much for us besides call the coast guard.

Another lobster-boat captain on the *Mya and Kibbly* was actually talking to my captain on the radio just before the windows were blown out. The very last words the *Mya and Kibbly* heard from our captain on the radio were "oh shit!" Considering my captain was very lucky, it was still light out enough to see the wave that hit the boat. He got on the floor in time; otherwise, he would have been decapitated.

The *Mya and Kibbly* stayed with us to ride the storm out for the night as we waited for the coast guard to show up. The seas were so bad that night, the main engine on the *Mya and Kibbly* actually stalled trying to climb a sea. I don't want to try to even imagine what that was like, climbing a sea so big that all you see is an enormous wall of water, and you can't see the top of the wave with no engine power.

I had a captain tell me once that the *Mya and Kibbly* was underpowered. (Dead in the water means to have no momentum or chance of progression. It is a nautical term that originally referred to a ship with a motionless sail on a windless day, which appeared to be dead in the water.) Now that gives it another meaning, doesn't it?

The following morning, the coast guard showed up to tow us back to Plymouth Harbor. The seas were diminishing as well as the wind. It was still challenging to get a tow rope aboard our boat to start towing us. The coast guard towed us to the entrance of Plymouth Harbor, and from there, we hobbled to the dock looking like a wounded battleship coming back from war.

There were about a dozen or more people at the dock waiting for us. I'll never forget that. A lot of them were the old-timers who greeted us when we came in from a fishing trip. We would give them some rock crab that we also caught in the lobster traps. In return, they would have their wives bake a cake or make some lasagna for the boat ride out to sea. I miss them; they had a great deal of respect for us.

Mike sailed the broken boat to Kelly's shipyard in Fairhaven, Massachusetts. I was out of work for a month before the boat was ready to go fishing again. After that trip, witnessing the power of a raging sea, I knew in my heart that some higher power had made this place. There is a God! There will always be books written. How do you explain the Egyptian army? They had logbooks for their army. How do you explain over one hundred thousand elite soldiers disappearing off the books? Oh yeah—Moses!

There were rumors about getting the boat fixed and taking it to Florida for the winter. There were three fisheries the owner wanted to try off the coast of Port Canaveral in Florida: wreckfish, golden tilefish, and golden crab.

Wreckfish are typically forty to sixty pounds and two and a half to four feet long but can reach a maximum of 220 pounds and six and a half feet in length. They have a long life span, with some living more than seventy years. They got their nickname because a lot of these fish make their homes around shipwrecks.

Golden tilefish are beautiful with colorful green and yellow markings. Tilefish can grow up to eighty pounds and up to four feet long. They live in family groups on the side of a muddy canyon and burrow holes in the mud with their mouths to make a home.

The golden crab is a large nonswimming crab with a golden cream shell. Adult males typically weigh between three and five pounds while the female is considerably smaller.

The *Adventure* was all fixed up and ready to go fishing again on the high seas. The owners decided to take the boat to Port Canaveral, Florida, with two hundred lobster traps to try and catch golden crabs. It was January, and I was looking forward to some warm tropical water. Say good riddance to freezing eyelashes from the bitter cold making your eyes water, and that was what the police in Plymouth was saying about me leaving with the boat for Florida.

The honest truth was that Crown Royal whisky didn't mix with a child that was raised part Ferrell. Point being, I was looking at a police officer with his arms sprawled and his eyes and mouth wide open, staring at me inside the jail cell. I was asking him in a deep voice, "What are you looking at?" I was on my knees, washing the blood off my face from the toilet bowl water. That night, I was trying to play *Underdog*, and I got protective custody by the Plymouth police. (*Underdog* is an old cartoon of a superhero dog that has a cape and flies around saving people, including his love, Polly Purebred, from the evil villain.)

Captain Mike knew that Captain Crunch and I didn't get along. That's why he sailed the boat and made Crunch drive the truck to Florida.

It took us almost a week to get to Port Canaveral, Florida. We stayed fifty to sixty miles off the eastern coastline to stay away from the strong Gulf Stream currents. (The current velocity is fastest near the surface of the Gulf Stream, with a maximum speed of 5.6 mph as it travels north. The Gulf Stream is a warm and swift Atlantic Ocean current that originates in the Gulf of Mexico and stretches to the tip of Florida and follows the eastern coastlines of the United States and Newfoundland before crossing the Atlantic Ocean.)

Mike took the boat as captain and made Captain Crunch drive his truck to Florida, and it was the best part of the trip for me. See what happens when men let their ego run rampant—they blow windows out of fishing boats!

When we finally got to Florida, I couldn't believe how many boats there were. There were at least seven boats abreast (boats tied up together side by side). Most of the boats were made of wood or fiberglass, and they were all shrimp and tilefish boats. The majority of the boats were pretty much tied up for the winter, and if and when you did make a trip, they would call it scraping (just enough to get by). I learned all this through a friend I made in Port Canaveral. His parents owned two shrimp boats, and they left him to watch the boats. Honestly, I was so drunk down there, I didn't remember his name!

They really weren't very happy to see a brand-new seventy-seven-foot steel boat pull up to the dock.

I remember Mike let us go recreational fishing for the day. Mike brought a ten-foot inflatable Zodiac with a twenty-five-horsepower outboard motor. It was very fast for a little boat. It could fit two to three people, and it was perfect to go recreational fishing deep into the harbor. Mike gave the whole crew a book on poisonous fish to read. That was just so he was not responsible for any deaths in case a greenhorn got poked and started foaming at the mouth.

There were all kinds of people from various areas living in their vans, more like those old Volkswagen bugs. Everybody had a cast net (a net in the shape of a circle with small weights all around it a foot apart, used to catch small baitfish). Everyone noticed we didn't have live bait and were more than happy to give us some.

I loved the Southern hospitality. Now I know why people up North and down south of Massachusetts call people in Massachusetts Massholes. And you know what? They're right. Living in Massachusetts is a setup for a heart attack! My father always told me, "Five people call you a horse, start looking for a saddle!"

Stress is the number one proxy killer disease today. The American Medical Association has noted that stress is the basic cause for more than 60 percent of all human illnesses and diseases around the world.

The next day was all business as usual. We had brought two hundred lobster traps with us in hopes of catching the golden crab. We had to unload one hundred lobster traps. There was a storage unit across the street from the boat that Mike had rented. People were in awe because we were working so hard and fast to unload the lobster traps. They have two speeds down South: slow and slower. That's the Southern pace. We left one hundred traps on the boat to take out to sea and try and catch the golden crab first. Well, considering we had no deck space left, the captain had no choice.

Mike had us going all over the place. Every time I looked at the loran to see how far we were going, it would say one hundred nautical miles. We ended up in the Bermuda Triangle, and the water was so unbelievably crystal clear. The salt that dried on the rail was one thousand times the size of table salt—no exaggeration. When you got seawater in your eyes, it burned something painful!

Mike decided to set out one trap 980 to 1,000 fathoms deep. Talk about crazy; that was one mile deep.

We put extra weights in each end of the trap then baited it up and threw it overboard with the longest end line I had ever made. Then we went to the shoal water to set two fifty-trap trawls while we let the gear soak (give the traps time to catch something). There was a huge longline drum on deck. It was basically the world's biggest fishing reel. The spool was four feet OD (outer diameter), and it was about five to six feet long with a huge level-wind (which made the wire go back and forth so it would go on the spool evenly, winding it back on the longline drum).

The idea was to drop the weight slowly until it hit the floor of the ocean and jig it up and down in a controlled motion. Well, picture this. The captain was being a blatherskite (silly, babbling speech that doesn't really mean anything). If you know someone who talks just to hear his or her own voice, you can call what he or she says blatherskite talk. I could picture in my mind what the fishing gear was going to look like!

When it came back to the surface, I was right and then some. It came back literally backward and in a big ball. Captain Crunch was in the engine room, still looking for his chest of gold!

Mike decided to go haul the trap that was 980 fathoms deep. I was excited to see what the trap caught one mile deep. It took forty-five minutes for the trap to reach the surface from the ocean floor.

When the trap landed on the rail, I couldn't believe what I was looking at inside the trap: a giant isopod. It looked like a huge sand flea. They get big—REALLY BIG. Typically, giant isopods are between 7.5 and 14.2 inches in length, but they can get much bigger. One isopod was caught two and a half feet long, weighing in at 3.7 lb. The isopod in the lobster trap was twelve inches long and just about one pound. It looked so prehistoric, no one dared to touch it!

I remember memorizing, looking at these isopods in books when I was a child, wondering if I'd ever get to see one someday. And not many people will ever see one of these in a lifetime.

I stepped right up to the plate and slowly opened the trapdoor. I nervously reached in, wondering if this was a good idea. I couldn't believe what I was holding—something I thought, as a child, I would never be able to see. In amazement, I turned around to show everyone as they backed up like I had leprosy. We saved the isopod for a scientist Mike knew at the dock.

We couldn't find the first fifty-trap trawl we set. Something wasn't right. Either we didn't put enough end line on or the high flyers got ran over by big ships, and their huge propellers chewed them up and spit them out.

When we got back to the second fifty-trap trawl, the Gulfstream was literally sucking the ball and high flyer under the water from all its power. I had to take the throw grapple and hook the high flyer's hat then grab the aluminum pole to tie another line on the ten-fathom piece. I cut the high flyer off, put the line in the hauler, and continued hauling the trawl. Sounds a hell of a lot easier on paper, I tell you! When you're hauling the trawl, there is 2,500 to 3,000 psi of strain on the line you're hauling! (A line is a rope. A real lobsterman on a boat calls it fishing line—5/8-inch-thick rope.)

When we hauled the trawl, to my shock, there were the same things in it as up north in Georges Bank. The water is so deep and cold that Jonah crabs and mud hake live down there too. (Mud hake is a bottom fish that lives on muddy bottoms, also known as trash fish.) I was disappointed we didn't catch a golden crab, but I was happy to be in the middle of nowhere in the warm Florida Gulf Stream!

We made one hundred traps in two fifty-trap trawls. One trawl is one mile worth of line, with a lobster trap every twenty-five fathoms connected to a 5/8-inch line with a half-inch, one-fathom piece of line tied to a bridle that's tied to the trap and spliced into the 5/8-inch main line. (Splice means to join or connect lines by interweaving the strands.)

Mike (deceased now) knew I was excited and screamed out the wheelhouse window, "Smile, Kyle! We're going to catch tile."

That always put a smile on my face. He was a good captain, and he always knew how to lift spirits up, not tear them down!

I said loudly with excitement, "Yes!" Then we set off to go tile-fishing for the next day.

Tilefishing is fun. We used a longline drum (the world's biggest fishing reel). I called it the world's biggest cheese slicer—point being, while you're hauling the longline gear back aboard the boat and you're going parallel, things (hopefully) will run nicely and smoothly. If you're hauling the gear back aboard the boat and you're going parallel and then suddenly you make a hard starboard and end up perpendicular, first, you will start seeing sparks shooting inboard like a Fourth of July Roman candle. Then that's when you know you're at the beginning of the end, and you're starting to cut the boat in half!

*****

We set ten miles of 3/8-inch wire cable and about five hundred hooks. A normal set would be about ten to fifteen miles of cable and fifteen hundred to two thousand hooks, depending on how good the fishing was.

After the end of the set, I was going to make an end line (a line connected to the cable with a weight that won't slide). But Mike was captain and knew it all, so I thought, *Well, Mike took a heavy weight and tied a snap on it.*

As soon as I figured what his intention was, I told him, "Noooo. Don't do that, Mike."

He said, "Shut up. I've been doing this before you were born."

Well, snaps are made to slide on the wire cable. So when Mike put a seventy-five-pound weight and snapped it on the wire and let it go, he looked at me as if to say, "Oh crap. The kid was right!"

We both stared and watched the weight slide down the cable until it disappeared. Then I acted like nothing happened. I finished setting up the wire cable with an end line, ball, and high flyer. What Mike did would have been fine if there was another end to pick up. Mike was too impatient with the first end we set out that he set a weight with no end line, ball, or high flyer to pick up. We only had a high flyer, ball, end line, and a weight that was going to slide ten miles to the other end with all the other five hundred hooks on it.

I didn't say a word. We ate lunch to let the gear soak to catch some fish.

Well, it was the longest lunch I'd ever eaten. Mike knew exactly what was in store when it was haul-back time, and he was nibbling small bites of his sandwich like a mouse. I didn't even want to go on deck. I offered to do the dishes and clean up after lunch. I tried to milk the dishes as long as I could (take my time). When I finally got geared up and went on deck, everyone was staring at the water, waiting for the hooks.

Everybody was wondering where the hooks were. But Mike and I knew damn well where they were. We got about maybe half a mile back before you could hear something let go in the wire, and then the wire went slack. I rushed to the rail, and when I looked overboard, I saw this big ball of hooks, monofilament, and a weight almost make it to the surface. The wire cable parted from all the strain. I watched a weight, a huge ball of monofilament, and hooks slowly descend into the abyss. (Monofilament was a type of fishing line using a single strand of man-made fiber.) We used a three-foot piece of monofilament. On one end was a hook, and on the other end was a snap that attached to the 3/8-inch wire cable.

When you put twenty-five miles of cable on the fishing spool, it's not one continuous twenty-five miles. You put it on a half mile to one mile at a time depending on how big of a spool you buy. Then you crimp (compress something into small folds or ridges). You crimp one end of the wire to the next spool of wire and continue putting the wire cable on the world's biggest fishing reel. The weight must have hit a crimp and pulled the two pieces of wire apart. Now everything we set out was lost: nine and a half miles of cable and five hundred hooks gone.

This guy reminded me of King Midas—everything he touched turned to gold. Well, it's the same thing, but everything he touched turned against him!

One thing I love most about tomorrows is that it's a new day. The next day is a fresh start, and whatever misery occurred the day before was behind me.

For whatever reason, there wasn't a lot of cable left on the long-line drum. There was maybe seven or eight miles (if that) left on the reel drum spool. So we made the best of it and set out whatever cable wire we could without spooling the drum. (Spooling all the wire comes of the drum completely—not good!)

Mike let me set up the next longline set and stayed inside the wheelhouse. The crew asked me what happened. I said, "I don't know." I didn't dare tell anyone the truth about what Mike did. Mike was the captain. I liked him, and he loved me.

Once, Mike said to me on a deck blowing forty-to-fifty-knot winds and twenty-to-thirty-foot seas, "Kyle, if I had four men like you on deck, I'd have the best crew in the whole fleet!"

Mike made his homemade spaghetti sauce. Everyone loved Mike's homemade sauce and meatballs! It took all day, and by the time dinner came around, you were ready to chew your arm off and eat it.

When we started hauling back, we were getting empty hooks, one after another. I was unsnapping the hooks off the cable and thinking where the hooks were on the ocean floor. I knew where and how tilefish lived.

Everyone on deck was pissed! I knew the hooks weren't on the tilefish yet, and I was hoping I was right. After a few more empty hooks, I saw this yellow-green white ball coming up the cable. Then Mike screamed out, "Bingo!" This huge thirty-to-forty-pound tilefish came out of the surface of the water and into my arms!

After that first one, every hook had a big tilefish. I mean BIG: forty-five-to-fifty-pounders. We made a couple of sets—rather small ones but very fruitful. We kept making small sets until we had about ten thousand pounds of tilefish. Mike decided to cut the trip short to get some more wire cable, hooks, monofilament, food, and fuel.

When we got to the dock, there were a lot of people looking at this beautiful seventy-seven-foot steel Gladding-Hearn. Most of them were boat owners and deckhands. Mike told me to ignore everyone on the dock and unload the fish.

The next day, all I heard was people talking about how we flooded the market and dropped the price to four dollars per pound from five dollars per pound off the boat. The other tilefish boats were ready to get their pitchforks and torches to scare off the ogre. They had good reason to. These smaller tilefishing boats were no competition for the Adventure The smaller boats would go out for the day and bring home maybe eight hundred to one thousand pounds, which was good for them because nobody flooded the market with too much fish.

The next day was all business. We loaded the boat with the last of the one hundred lobster traps we brought with us and spooled more wire on the longline drum. It seemed like the trips went downhill from there. All the wood traps were lost from the Gulf Stream. That's what Mike thought. I think those tilefish boats cut all our ends off because we kept catching more tilefish than the market could handle, making the price of tilefish drop dramatically.

It was springtime back in New England, and I had just about enough of Captain Crunch. Mike knew it also and had to make a decision. The situation was getting uglier and uglier day by day. Finally, Captain Crunch decided to let me go. His bottom lip was quivering from fear because he was so afraid of me! I had no quarrels. I knew I needed to move on to better pastures, and the state police were coming to the boat asking questions, and one of them was "Is he crazy?"

Mike decided to do the right thing. He bought me a plane ticket back to New England and said, "I'll call you when the boat gets back to Plymouth, Massachusetts. And please stay out of trouble, Kyle. You're a good man—just a little fucked up in the head, that's all."

When I got back to Plymouth, I knew my heart would never leave New England.

Mike had a hard time in Florida. Everybody quit and Mike had to fly someone to Florida to help take the boat back to Plymouth.

I ran into Jimmy, and he told me Ron Howard bought a $1.2-million lobster boat. It was the nicest lobster boat on the East Coast. Jimmy said he changed his ways big time, and he was a new man. I was also told by a fisherman, "All fishermen lie except me and you, and I don't know about you!"

The *Adventure* made it back to port with no crew. What happened next surprised me. Joe became Ron Howard's full-time captain and took Ron's whole crew to go run the *Adventure*. Now Ron Howard had no captain and no crew. I wasn't really thrilled about working for Joe or Ron for that matter. So I figured I'd call Ron to see what he had to say.

Ron wasn't very happy with Joe at all. He told me he treated his men very fairly now, and he'd give me a full share. He sounded convincing or, basically, desperate. So I gave Ron Howard another shot.

When I saw the boat, I fell in love her. It was named *Mechelle Le* after his daughter. She was seventy-seven feet long and twenty-two feet wide with a lobster tank that could hold twenty thousand pounds of lobster and a fishhold that could hold fifty thousand pounds of fish. It had a walk-in freezer aft of the fishhold that stored lobster bait to keep the redfish bait fresh from the hot summer heat.

I was about twenty-four or twenty-five years old by now. I wasn't a kid anymore, and I definitely could hold my own, especially in a bar fight. I didn't care how many men there were. I'd take them all on. I didn't care one iota. After you've been hit with rogue waves at least seventy to eighty feet high at sea, it changes you a lot! (Rogue waves—or freak or killer waves—have been part of marine folklore for centuries but have only been accepted as real by scientists over the past few decades. Most reports of extreme storm waves say they look like "walls of water." They are often steep-sided with unusually deep troughs.)

A lot of people thought I was kind of crazy. In actuality, I was very smart. I made them think I was crazy. Everybody stayed away from me. My father told me, "Would you rather be feared or loved by strangers, not by family?" Hence, seeing my brother whipped with a dog chain summed up my father's parenting ethics. One good thing I was taught early in life, it's not how good you can hit, it's how good you can take a punch, kick, or both!

The crew was Don, Tim, Clark, and me. Don was from the Cape, kind of like a yuppie fisherman. He would have his foul-weather gear dry-cleaned. That's Cape Cod for you. Tim was a smart-mouth who always had a smart remark. Clark was in a league all by himself. He had been swordfishing with Steve Howard (Ron's father) for ten years.

It was spring, and I missed the winter—well, at least the worst part anyway. But then again, I couldn't forget about what happened in November blowing the windows out either.

I loved the *Mechelle Le*. What a boat it was to work on: a house on the water. Ron figured if you're going to spend the better part of eight months a year on the water, you might as well be comfortable. I mean, it had central air conditioning, a state-of-the-art stereo system on deck, a saltwater ice machine, and a longline drum for swordfish and tuna fish on the overhead. There was another longline drum for groundfish on deck. The overhead longline drum had forty miles of floating 800-pound test monofilament, where the longline drum for groundfish had twenty miles of 3/8-inch wire to sink on the bottom. They call fish that live on the bottom floor of the ocean groundfish.

Ron was taking the boat full-time, seeing as how his captain left and took his whole crew with him. Out of my whole career offshore fishing, this was the longest crew that I'd been with—a total of five years with the same crew.

We teamed up in pairs. Basically, it was Don and me against Tim and Clark Kent. One thing I liked about Clark was that he hated Joe. They were in love with the same girl, Anna Hail. Joe ended up marrying Anna.

According to Clark, they wouldn't talk to each other for a whole month while out to sea fishing together. It takes seven days to get to the fishing grounds and then fourteen days to swordfish with no sleep. There's plenty of time to sleep on the way home—seven days back to the beach. (The Grand Banks are a group of underwater plateaus southeast of Newfoundland on the North American continental shelf. These areas are relatively shallow, ranging from eight fathoms deep to fifty fathoms in depth.)

I do remember having a few good times on the *Mechelle Le*—until I got my paycheck anyway. Ron and his father were well known for having a sharp pencil (screwing you on your paycheck)!

We went sword and tuna fishing in Georges Bank. (Georges Bank is a large elevated area of the sea floor between Cape Cod, Massachusetts, and Cape Sable Island, Nova Scotia. It separates the

Gulf of Maine from the Atlantic Ocean. The origin of its name is obscure.)

We caught a lot of bluefin. I remember they were good-sized too, about seven hundred to one thousand pounds. (Well, considering bluefin can historically reach weights of up to two thousand pounds and lengths of nearly fifteen feet. The Atlantic bluefin tuna is the largest tuna and easily the largest species in the mackerel family.) It was the biggest damn fish I'd ever seen or dreamed of ever seeing besides the brook trout I used to catch behind my house growing up as a child!

We caught some swordfish too. But the best fish (my favorite) is the mahi-mahi: the most beautiful fish in the ocean. There are two other names: dolphin and dorado. Not the dolphin flipper. Those are mammals that breathe air. Mahi-mahi is the Hawaiian name for this species (*Coryphaena hippurus*). It is also known as the dorado in Spanish or the dolphin fish in English. They turn all different colors right in front of your eyes. They are distinguished by dazzling colors—golden on the sides and bright blues and greens on the sides and back. The pectoral fins of the mahi-mahi are iridescent blue. Mahi-mahi are carnivorous, feeding on flying fish, crabs, squid, mackerel, and other forage fish. They have also been known to eat zooplankton. They're the most delicious fish you'll ever eat. In Hawaii, they eat mahi-mahi for breakfast. When you catch one on rod and reel, the mahi-mahi will tail walk (they walk on water with their tails on top of the water).

I remember one trip in March, I caught the biggest flounder I had ever seen!

The Atlantic halibut is the world's largest flatfish. The IGFA record was apparently broken off the waters of Norway in July 2013 by a 500-pound, eight-foot, seven-inch halibut. In July 2014, a 482-pound Pacific halibut was caught in Glacier Bay, Alaska. This is, however, discounted from records because the halibut was shot and harpooned before being hauled aboard. That is the Alaskan way to fish: harpoon and shoot the fish after you already caught it! I think maybe the crew got attacked by too many bears. Not sure but I'm still trying to figure that one out.

There is a secret canyon where colossal halibut run through in the early spring fishing at depths of 350 to 450 fathoms. We were groundfishing for hake, cusk, cod, and tilefish. We'd bring ten thousand pounds of mackerel for bait and actually use it all up in ten days, so we were averaging one thousand pounds of mackerel to cut up between the crew per day. We would cut up the mackerel in one-inch pieces. We were like those Japanese Ginsu chefs, cutting really fast by the winter's end.

In Newfoundland, they called these halibut sets shack sets. I found whole red crabs in the belly of halibut as well as mud hake and silver hake. Being strong swimmers, halibut are able to eat a large variety of fishes, including cod, turbot, pollack, and some invertebrates such as octopus, crab, and shrimp. Sometimes halibut leave the ocean bottom to feed on pelagic fish, such as salmon, sand lance, and herring, and even seal remains have been found in their stomachs. The sets were short (one mile for the end line), and we'd fish four to five miles on the sea floor of the canyon three hundred to four hundred fathoms deep. We'd then put another one-mile end line on the last end with high flyer and ball attached to the 3/8-inch cable-wire fishing line.

A captain told me once how he thought halibut killed their food. It's interesting. Picture this: a five-hundred-pound doormat pounding down on you out of nowhere. I think I confirmed this when I found a whole red crab in an enormous four-to-five-hundred-pound halibut's belly—crushed, flattened, and whole. It was flattened like something jumped on the red crab and swallowed it whole! I know, out of all the halibut we caught, there was at least one record halibut, but none were recorded. Unfortunately, now it's just a memory and a folklore to tell my children's children and their children and so on!

I like the way swordfish eat the best. The swordfish have been clocked up to sixty to eighty miles per hour. Swordfish is a popular seafood and another fast-leaping species, although its speed is not well known. One calculation determined that they could swim at sixty miles per hour, while other findings claimed speeds of over eighty miles per hour! The swordfish jets through the school at top speed, swishing its sword. Then the swordfish comes back around to see what it has killed or maimed.

There have been very few reports of swordfish attacks on humans, and none have resulted in death. Although there are no reports of unprovoked attacks on humans, swordfish can be very dangerous when provoked, and they can jump and pierce their swords into their targets. Here, a doctor from Malaysia describes an unusual case of death that resulted from intracranial penetrating injury caused by a swordfish. Here is the case report:

> A thirty-nine-year-old fisherman was attacked by a swordfish, which jumped toward him and pierced his right eye when he flashed a torch light at the water from his fishing boat. He was immediately rushed to the nearby hospital by his companion. Clinical examination revealed a swollen right eye with penetrating wound at the upper eyelid. He was later referred to our hospital for the apparent upper eye injury. However, on arrival at the hospital, about twenty hours after the incident, he became unconscious with a Glasgow Coma Scale of 7. [The Glasgow Coma Scale is often used to help define the severity of the brain injury. Mild head injuries are generally defined as those associated with a GCS score of 13 to 15, and moderate head injuries are those associated with a GCS score of 9 to 12. A GCS score of 8 or less defines a severe head injury.] He was intubated [inserting a tube through the mouth and then into the airway to assist breathing with a ventilator], and the computer [tomography scan or X-ray or ultrasound] showed proptosis [abnormal protrusion or displacement of an eye or other body part] of the right eye with subarachnoid hemorrhage [denoting or occurring in the fluid-filled space around the brain between

> through which major blood vessels pass]. He was ventilated for cerebral protection and covered with intravenous antibiotic. Unfortunately, the patient deteriorated rapidly with hypotension [abnormally low blood pressure].

The man succumbed one day after admission. The cause of death from postmortem examination was impalement of the head by swordfish. There are no reports of unprovoked swordfish attacks on humans, though there have been several reports of attacks resulting in body and chest injuries. This is the first report of a swordfish attack where the patient succumbed to death. The attack was possibly provoked by the flashing light, which the fish thought to be food. It was very unfortunate that the sword penetrated through the man's eye socket into his brain.

The swordfish snout elongates into a true sword shape. The upper jaw measures at least one-third the length of the body. It is long, flat, pointed, and very sharp. The average fish caught in the commercial fishery weighs between 90 kilograms or 100 pounds and 150 kilograms or 330 pounds. Swordfish are pelagic (living within the upper water column rather than on the bottom or in coastal areas). They are frequently found basking on the surface and are well known for their powerful jumping. They feed daily, most often at night when they rise to the surface and near-surface waters in search of smaller fish. They have been observed moving through schools of fish, thrashing their swords to kill and then quickly turning to consume their catch.

Swordfish attacks on humans are extremely rare, but they can kill if vital organs are involved. Do not underestimate the outcome of injuries caused by this fish. The attack was possibly provoked by the flashing light, which the fish thought to be food. Hence, it is suggested that fishermen should avoid flashing lights onto the surface of the water or stay away from the light source in order to avoid a similar tragedy.

Captain Ron was still Ron, but I do not know if I could ever forgive him. Ron respected my work ethic, but he didn't respect me for being a human being. His father, Steve Howard, was no better. I think it's about time someone told the truth about what happened years ago on those boats this father and son owned!

Joe told my brother Antonio, out of all the abuse he'd seen in his fishing career, Kyle got it the worst. But I stuck it out. My grandmother and mom always told me with a stern voice, "Never give up!" My grandmother always told me this when I was a little boy growing up. Whispering in my ear with bad breath, she'd say, "When you come to the end of your rope, tie a knot and hang on!"

Joe ended up naming his kid after me. The captain of the *Liam Bull* stopped his fork from going into his mouth while eating lunch out to sea. He couldn't conceive the idea that they didn't give me water for a day. He looked me square in the eyes as I sat across from him at the galley table. He told me I should own that big blue boat—meaning the *Michelle Le*.

Clark told me a story that made me realize people need to break the chain of abuse. The *Anna Bo* was swordfishing in the Grand Banks. Steve Howard was the captain, and Clark was on deck. The captain saw a piece of eight-hundred-pound test monofilament floating, and it went under the boat. Captain Steve took the boat out of gear and asked a deckhand if it cleared the propeller of the boat. He said the monofilament was all clear.

Well, it wasn't, and it got in the propeller. Steve got over the loud-hailer and asked the deckhand to wrap that monofilament line around his hand. Then Steve asked the man, "You got that line wrapped around your hand real good?"

The man said yes.

Then Steve put the boat in gear. The man went flying over to the rail, and the eight-hundred-pound test monofilament line parted and broke his hand.

I asked Clark what happened after that. He said that the man dropped to his knees, and his eyes were like water sprinklers. He held his hand up and screamed, "That fucking asshole!" Now he was fifteen hundred miles from the beach. What was he going to do about it besides stab the captain and throw him overboard? He would be bleeding out for the sharks to get a scent of his blood, and they could watch the sharks tear his limbs off! No, of course not. He was probably running from the law or didn't have a green card to work in the USA.

People often wonder why I put up with all that abuse. Well, it doesn't take a rocket scientist to figure that one out. My brother Antonio hitchhiked to California twice (back and forth) by the time he was seventeen years old. I've seen him whipped by a dog chain, and he looked like a cricket rubbing his legs together so fast that I was waiting for the noise.

You wonder what happened to Antonio to make him run away from home so young. Well, after seeing my brother Antonio whipped with a dog chain, it didn't look very fun watching the flesh disappear where the links of the dog chain met his flesh. I'll tell you that much!

I remember my mother and all my aunts sitting at my grandmother's house around the kitchen table. My uncle was sitting in the corner of the kitchen in a rocking chair. My mom started telling a story about a boy that was her cousin who rode his bicycle from RI all the way to Wareham, MA. She continued saying one of the neighbours said something bad about the boy. Once my mom's dad heard, he brough the boy in the basement and whipped him bloody! My youngest aunt scream out really loud, trying to talk because she was laughing so hard! He just didn't whip him; he tied him upside down! While she was slapping her hand on her thigh laughing! Then, my uncle who was sitting in the rocking chair, started to move the chair back and forth really slow. He took his hand, removed a toothpick from his mouth and said, "Yup, I cut him down."

Now I realize what I was taught had to be stopped or I'd teach my kids the wrong way. Breaking the chain of abuse is nothing to joke about literally. The first step is to start loving yourself and forgiving others and yourself.

Ron worked us like sled dogs in Alaska! I didn't care; it just made me strong as a bull. I kept talking about Alaska, and I really wanted to go. Ron said, "Give me a few more years to get you ready."

By that time, Clark and Tim were totally under my skin, and I needed a change. The boat *Anna* was at Dicky's Wharf in Massachusetts. I heard they were going to Cape May, New Jersey, to go offshore lobstering, and his father, Steve Howard, needed an experienced crew. I told Ron I was going to Alaska, but first, I was making a few trips on the *Anna*. Ron told me that his father was excited that I wanted to go fishing with him on his boat.

Steve Howard was taking the boat as captain. Steve had hired a girl, Captain Josie. She broke her ankle side setting lobster traps and was home healing up. (Side setting means setting traps on the midship starboard side of a boat. It is a dangerous way to set traps.)

I called Steve Howard to secure my site on his boat. He sounded very excited to have me aboard his boat to go fishing. He wanted to leave as soon as possible. He was behind schedule because he needed a crew, and he wanted someone with experience moving the lobster gear.

The day came to meet the crew and get the boat ready to go fishing. When I got to the boat, I'd never seen so many greenhorns on a boat at once. There were five or six greenhorns and just one experienced man—me! I couldn't understand it until I remembered Ron telling me his father only needed one good guy to rail that trap aboard! He could care less what happened after that. He always worked until someone got hurt bottom line!

My father told me, "If five people call you a horse, start looking for a saddle." And I could tell you that this guy wasn't as hard as my father was on me! He tried that crap with me, and a four-foot-tall, three-foot-wide oak lobster trap came flying into the hauler block and exploded into splinters. Then one of the two seventy-five-pound steel weights skimmed the top of my baseball cap as soon as I ducked, watching it come right square at my face!

I swear I grew horns in my head. I screamed into the loud-hailer, "If you do that again, I'm going to cut your f——n' heart out!"

I'm cursed with good hearing. Why? Some things in life you wish you never heard before!

After the trip, Steve was talking to his son on the dock, and he said to his son, "That Kyle. Oh boy. That Kyle, he has one hell of a temper, I'll tell ya!"

No wonder why he couldn't find anyone good but greenhorns anymore. I figured this man was going to take as many guys as he could, just in case some of the men didn't work out.

It was mid-February, and lobster prices were $7.50 per pound. It was a big secret that year (1993) that we were going offshore of Cape May, New Jersey.

Steve Howard had all his lobster gear in Georges Bank and needed to move it all down offshore of Cape May, New Jersey. At dinner, we were talking about how much gear we could put on the boat. Steve said ten trawls were the most he's ever put on her back. That was five hundred lobster traps. At the beginning of the trip, everybody had no idea what we were in for except for Captain Steve and me. When Steve said "five hundred traps," I waited for the expressions on the greenhorns' faces. They were all the same. A few of them stopped as their forks were going into their mouths, and their eyes opened wide. That was exactly what the captain of the *Liam Bull* did when I told him they didn't give me water for a day on the *Sea Slave*!

I looked at it one trap at a time. That was all my mind could handle—no more, no less!

Steve didn't care if he only had one guy that could rail the lobster traps, and that was all he could do. That's all he did on that trip. As long as that trap got aboard, that was all he cared about! Steve would scream into the loud-hailer, "Get that trap aboard!"

I've never heard anybody scream or yell so loud that it actually made my ears ring.

He wasn't screaming at me. I was standing next to a greenhorn who had no idea where the bit was on the bow. (A bit is a solid column that is sometimes square and sometimes cylindrical. It has a crossbar that is of lesser diameter and forms a lowercase letter *t*. These are also called Samson posts because they are so strong. You tie to them with a hitch around the crossbar, or they accept a loop line as well.)

All I kept thinking about when he was screaming at this greenhorn was a story Clark told me of how he saw a deckhand get screamed at for half an hour. He timed it. And for what did he get screamed at for? He lost the cap to a WD-40 can. (WD-40 is a lubricant for rusty nuts on bolts.) All these horrible stories I've heard about this man, yet I still went fishing with him. It was a scary feeling for a brief moment!

We didn't even have the first load of gear aboard to bring to Cape May. Suddenly, over the loud-hailer, I heard Steve say, "We have some weather coming." So I got a really good idea.

"Kyle, why don't you stack the gear? That way there. I'll know it's done right."

So I did—fifty traps bridle aft, fifty traps bridle forward. This was so the gear didn't get mixed up, and you would know where the last trap was to be set out. This was called the end trap.

Well, I did that for five hundred traps. It was the hardest I'd ever pushed myself. Not only did I stack. After the trawl was over with, there was one mile of line to pull in the fishhold to make room to haul another trawl. I couldn't believe how strong his lungs were and how loud of a pitch he could make, looking at him scream at a greenhorn pulling line, "You're about as strong as cat piss!"

I did more laughing on that boat than I did my whole career on any other boat I had ever worked on. So I hopped down the hole and pulled the line into the fishhold.

I could hear Steve say, "That's the way, Kyle. That's the way." He was all excited and smiling at me!

One of the greenhorns asked me, "How the hell do you keep working so hard? You're a freak of nature!"

I got mad at first and said, "What did you call me?"

The greenhorn actually was from the state of Maine. I don't remember his name, but he had no problem holding his own given the situation he was in. In a deep Maine accent, he said, "Up in Maine, that means a compliment."

I apologized and told him, "It's all in the mind." Then I laughed at him and walked away.

The truth is I read this article about an Olympian that won a gold medal. He was a rower in one of those long canoes. He was the captain of the team, and he was talking about physical pain while he was rowing long distances. He said, "Well, the best way to explain it was when you can't row anymore, and your arms are tired, and they are stinging from pain. Don't think about it. Block it out of your mind."

It takes practice, but this man was right. It's all in the mind. If you believe, you will prevail! Don't think of the pain; block it out of your mind.

After thirty years of doing this, I had mastered it. It is the same for exercising the brain. If you are a lefty, do things with your right hand. *20/20* did a documentary on it decades ago. My father was always calling me to watch the TV show *20/20*. They said if you use the opposite side of your brain that you don't use, you will make it stronger. I had been doing this for years before they did that documentary.

Captain Don on the *Mechelle Le* doesn't believe I'm a lefty and probably still does not believe me till this day. I would hold the lobster with my left hand and band it with my right hand. I am left-handed. It was not easy, I tell you, but I perfected it. Well, there wasn't much else to do. I stabbed my good banding hand, and trips were almost one thousand dollars per day. So I had no choice but to go offshore and work, work, work, work, and do more work and maybe even a lot more work!

I liked what Stanley said to me once on the *Sea Slave*. Now, he worked for the hardest captain there was, and if he figured out something to tolerate unspeakable things, then there must be something to it. It was the end of the trip, and I was taking bait out of the fishhold, and bait juice was dripping on me. We ended the trip, and we had extra bait to throw overboard. I was all pissed off when Stanley told me, "Don't think about it." I will remember that for the rest of my life.

As much as I don't want to admit it, Joe had a good one. "Don't get mad, get better!

After we got all five hundred traps aboard, I went in, cleaned up, and cooked some grub up. We were talking about the gear and the boat. I told Steve I think we had room for two or three more trawls aboard the boat. Steve just about spit out his milk with his little bit of Coca Cola he'd mixed into it from a greenhorn's fresh cold soda that he just cracked open. The greenhorns looked at me like I was crazy and wanted to stab me with their forks and knives. I wasn't sure.

Steve, really loudly, said to me, "You think so, Kyle? You think so?" He was smiling from ear to ear. "Well, I'll give you first watch, and we'll talk about it!"

The wheelhouse on the *Anna* was awesome. You were really high above the ocean surface. It gave me a greater sense of security being in the big wheelhouse, looking down at the porpoises catch a free ride off the wake of the enormous bow cutting through the seawater. Then there was a water bubbler—the tall ones, like in high school.

Steve was funny. He loved that water bubbler just as much as I did. He loved talking about the water bubbler too. He told me that while he was in the shipyard, he would run right over to the spot where he was standing when he got the idea. Then he'd finish telling me about being in the shipyard. He said, "I was real thirsty one day and thought it would be great to have a drink of water." Then he got the great idea to put a water bubbler in. And he walked over to it, taking a real long drink from it.

Then he would talk about finding good men, and I'd tell Steve there weren't any left to get a rise out of him. He would say, "Stop scaring me like that, Kyle. It's not true." Then he'd get upset.

We set all the gear and were on our way back to Georges Bank to load the boat up again. This time, twelve trawls aboard and twelve miles of line and traps.

Every time we had a steam back to Cape May or Georges Bank, Steve loved tidying up the boat. I remember going into the galley, and Steve had a large metal spoon electric-taped to a three-foot-long and two-inch-wide wood-bottom lathe from a lobster trap. He told me to go to the engine room and give this spoon to a young man with curly black hair. So I went to the engine room to find five greenhorns cleaning and scrubbing. The engine room was huge, so I walked over to the other side, slowly looking around. I couldn't find the curly-haired greenhorn. The next thing I knew, I felt a tap on my calf. To my shock, I jumped a little when I saw him.

He was unrecognizable from so much grease in his hair, face, teeth, and clothes. He needed the spoon to scrape the bilge under the main engine. Still to this day, I say to myself, "What the heck!" when I think of that kid.

Steve had a great deal of respect for me.

When we finally got all the gear off the boat side setting, we started hauling lobster gear right away. I couldn't believe it. We were catching anywhere from five hundred to nine hundred pounds of lobster out of fifty traps.

I remember Steve telling me on the second night, "Kyle, scream at them. Kyle, scream at them. I can't scream anymore."

So I told the greenhorns to just go with it. "I'm going to pretend to scream, but don't let him see you laugh or even smile."

It worked great, and we had some fun, except for the poor bastards that had to stack. They couldn't band because they were getting bit so badly, they had tears in their eyes. It hurts to get bit by a five-pound lobster's crusher claw.

One kid sounded like he was having sex with the lobster. He had a good five-pound lobster with the crusher claw right across his fingers. All I could hear was "Ahahhaaaaa! Hahaha! Ohoooooaa! Oohohohhoh myyy god!" The greenhorn's face was toward the sky, and his eyes rolled up way in his head.

I remember one day, a greenhorn was pushing a trap down the rail, and it fell on deck. I didn't know who weighed more—him or the trap. So I picked the trap up, and to my surprise, there were a few more lobsters in one end of the trap. I asked him, "Why are those lobsters in the trap still?"

And the greenhorn replied with some shortness of breath, "I figured we were catching enough of them." He was all wide-eyed and had what I call culture shock. He said, "Please don't tell Steve."

I was laughing so hard, I couldn't talk.

Then he said, "I knew you were crazy."

I took the lobsters back to the banding table to share a laugh with Kato, who was standing there the whole trip, banding and getting bit.

At the end of the night, I'd get in the habit of racing in the galley. I would grab the ice cream while running to the table, slap a scoop or two in the bowl, and then I'd sit down and eat it slowly.

You could hear footsteps really fast coming down the stairs from the wheelhouse. It would be Steve. "You beat me again, Kyle. You beat me to the ice cream again." All excited, he would talk about the good lobster run we had that day.

My first trip on the *Anna*, we caught seventeen thousand pounds of lobster. Steve was to make a few more trips, and then I was on my way to Alaska.

The trips went by fast, and so did the men. Especially on payday—if you want to call it that. The same thing applied to Steve as it did to Ron. Well, I wonder where Ron got the idea from now. Steve withheld a paycheck so you didn't get paid until the next trip. He would hand out the envelopes then hightail it, waddling to his truck to leave. That was when the swearing began. He paid me $3,000, and he paid the other men $500. I acted like my paycheck was like theirs and started stomping my foot and swearing too.

What was I supposed to do? I couldn't just say, "Oh boy. I made $3,000. Well, see you guys later."

In actuality, I was mad because my real share should have been $7,500. One captain told me that if it was his boat, the share would have been 9 percent instead of Steve's 5 percent full share.

I went to the boat the next day and confronted Steve about my share. He basically started backing up to the wheelhouse because of my screaming. Steve kept saying, "I don't need you! I don't need you!"

So I calmed down and talked calmly. He actually said, "If I give you their share that you worked for, will you stand behind me at the dock when I tell the men?"

I said yes and walked away.

He yelled out, "Where are you going now?"

I told him, "I'll be back leave day. I'm going to New Hampshire, Lake Winnipesaukee, to catch a lake trout ice fishing!"

That's exactly what I did. I drove straight to New Hampshire. I got a room and went to the bait and tackle store. I spent $400 on gear and went ice fishing. You were only allowed two holes on the ice, so there was no need to buy an ice auger.

So I bought this handheld auger. I think it was twenty-four-inch hole. Anyways, it took me forty-five minutes to break through the ice. It was three feet thick. I was down to a T-shirt by the end of the two holes I was allotted.

I did this for two days. Finally, the man in the tackle store said, "Hey, kid. Buy this book. I'll show you where to catch some fish."

After walking back into his cozy warm tackle store again (but this time to buy ice cleats), a gust of wind blew me, and I slid backward ten to fifteen feet. I turned around, and I was looking at miles of open clear ice. So I slowly made my way to the shoreline, praying for no gust of wind to blow me across the lake. I was thinking to myself that I must be putting on a great show for this man, considering his tackle store was right across the street, in front of where I was fishing. What did I have to lose but another twenty dollars?

It was a book on New Hampshire lakes. He showed me a lake called Ossipee Lake, where he owned a house on the shoreline. The gentleman told me if I wanted to catch a rainbow trout, I'd have to see the bottom of the pond, so I should fish close to the shoreline.

He added, "But be careful of the dam, especially if you're planning to drive your truck on the lake. The closer you get to the dam, the thinner the ice gets from underwater currents."

You were allowed five fishing traps on Ossipee Lake, so I got there early at 2:00 a.m. I know it was early, but you were allowed to have five holes in the ice, and it was going to take till daybreak to get them all drilled out, and it would also keep me warm.

It was great for the tackle shop because I had to buy three more ice-fishing traps. The man was nice enough to give me free bait—and plenty of it too.

It was so cold that morning, walking to the spot where he told me to fish, that my eyelashes were freezing together. The bait was kept in a foam bucket inside a five-gallon bucket so the water didn't freeze. By the time I'd grabbed a minnow and put the baitfish on my hook, it was already frozen. I had to take the minnow and put it under the water and hook it on underwater.

I had the best day ever ice fishing. I have never had a better day yet, but I'm still going to damn well try!

I heard that Josie was coming back soon. Steve nicknamed her Hurdy, and I have no idea why.

Steve took the boat and probably decided that it was his last trip. I'm not sure. It wasn't your normal trip. People were getting hurt on the rail to the point where everybody was afraid to rail traps aboard. I was the last one that, basically, wasn't afraid to rail. As for Kato's hand, I'm surprised it wasn't crushed.

I don't know if Steve knew what he was doing or not. I sure let him know! He wasn't paying attention or he was a very sick man, taking traps and running them into the block. Kato's hand was grabbing the top post of the lobster trap to rail it. Well, the trap kept going and sandwiched his hand between the trap and the block. The trap splintered into nothing; there was just twine hanging. Kato fell back. He stood up then fell on his knees, holding his left hand. His eyes were like water sprinklers, wide open and staring at me like "what the fuck!"

I told him, "Don't look at it. It's not bleeding. The pain will go away." Then I told him to get some frozen vegetables out of the freezer to numb his hand to the point where it hurt again! Then all I could hear was "I'm not railing! Fuck you!"

"No, fuck you! You rail!"

"No, you rail! Fuck you. I'm not railing."

We were bickering at each other.

The greenhorns had this terrified look on their faces like an "I just want to go home now" look. I felt for them. I knew this job sucked when I first started. I remember rage like I never felt before take over me!

Another trap almost went up into the block. I power-railed it so it didn't go into the block. I didn't mind that.

It was the end trap with two huge steel bars on each end that I minded. The trap came up flying into the block. I realized I should listen to my instincts saying, "I'm not power-railing this trap."

As soon as I backed off the trap, one of the two seventy-five-pound steel weights went flying over my head. I felt it skim across the very top of my head.

Steve said over the loud-hailer, "Oh, I thought the end trap was aboard already."

The next thing I knew, I was levitating off the deck. With a demonic voice, I told him, "If you ever do that again, I'm going to take my Dexter [six-inch carbon-bladed knife] and cut your fucking heart out and squish it in my bare fucking hands and watch it ooze out of my fingers."

Those were my exact words!

He didn't say a word the rest of the trip. Steve Howard had finally met his match when it came to any more deck abuse! There comes a point in one's life where you can't and will not put up silent boundaries anymore!

The greenhorns were dumbfounded. It's the best way I could put it. But I was adamant on what I did or said… I was going to do! He gave me a lot more respect, I'll tell you that, in March 1993 off Cape May, New Jersey!

Well, like I said earlier, Captain Josie came the next trip with an unhealed broken ankle. She actually brought a portable leg exercise machine to strengthen her ankle. I met Josie once in Gloucester. I was carrying this small bag of Black Beauty (an eighty-pound bag of black sandblast) as I was ready to climb a ladder to the *Mechelle Le* that was dry-docked at the time. She walked by and said a quick remark: "The bag is a lot heavier than it looks. Ha. She said it with a big bubbling smile.

All I kept thinking was *She's too cute to be a captain. What the hell was she thinking?*

I was happy because Sean Cob (deceased) was going on the trip. He just got back from Alaska, fishing for black cod. If you want to have anybody on deck with the best work attitude you can ever imagine, it's Sean Cob.

Well, actually, after black cod fishing, Sean went to work for his fishing mate, whom he worked on deck with. The guy owned a salmon boat and had a license handed down to him from generation to generation.

Sean kept saying he thought he was the cat's ass and put up with his ego. Sean finally had enough, and at the end of the day, while they were winding down and having a few beers, the infamous truth serum took over Sean. He told the guy what he really thought of him. That he wasn't half the man that he thinks he is, and Sean knew fishermen back here in the East Coast that would work him under the table.

Well, that ended that job. Then he decided to come back to New England to go fishing and ended up with me on the *Anna*.

I was ready for a change. A girl captain—how easy of a trip can you get?

Josie was just like one of the guys. She was funny and had such a positive attitude, she was overflowing, bubbling with it. She gave off a great aura about herself.

Sean brought some videos of Alaska to show us on the steam to Cape May, New Jersey. I was excited to see them, as was everyone else. The video showed Sean midship starboard side at the hauling station, opening a big sliding door to an all-enclosed three-hundred-foot fishing machine. As soon as he opened the sliding door, the view and sound alone of the huge waves breaking was enough to make a greenhorn fall to the deck in the fetal position and start sucking his thumb!

One thing all longline captains love is no matter how bad the weather gets—and this goes for top fish gear and bottom fish gear captains—you're still going on deck!

I couldn't believe the weather; only professional sea legs could handle being in conditions like that. A greenhorn would end up looking like the semi-experienced greenhorn losing his horns, cartwheeling right into the prop wash right in front of my eyes. (Prop wash is a current of water created by the action of a propeller or rotor.) If that ever happened in Alaska or in the Bering Sea, there was no way you were coming back alive. Even worse, you're midship and you might get sucked into the propeller.

Sean's job was at the rail, unsnapping longline gear and landing the fish onto a conveyer belt that led into the belly of the ship to the process workers, where they cleaned and froze the black cod fish.

When I said "how easy of a trip can you get," I didn't mean workwise. I meant socially. After being out to sea for decades, you miss out on a lot. I'm not talking about sex either. I'm talking about just that talking with the opposite sex, or just their being there is incredible! Things you appreciate a lot more, like just a conversation with a woman (and not a sexual one either). I'm the youngest out of eight kids (four boys and four girls), so I grew up with girls in the house.

I grew up Catholic, went to Sunday school, made my confirmation, and no, nothing happened to me either! I think she reminded me of my older sisters. They left the house early in life, so I think, subconsciously, she was probably filling in. Like I found out, like we all do on things that we're lacking from our childhood!

We didn't bring as many men for this trip. For an experienced crew, all you need is three good men. We brought four men. It was to be a long trip. There was talk about letting the gear soak and going groundfishing or maybe tuna fishing.

There was a computer aboard that could tell you the water temperature anywhere around the world. The Cape May water temperature was 75 degrees. There were a few more trawls to pick up at Georges Bank, and then we were off to Cape May, New Jersey. We loaded the gear and headed right back to Cape May to start lobstering.

After we set the gear and started hauling, there was a noticeable difference in the catch. The lobsters had dropped off quite a bit. I really didn't mind because the talk about going tuna fishing or groundfishing was exciting to me, and we could make a decent trip out of it.

I remember Josie saying we had some bad weather coming. Josie asked Steve on the radio if she could port in at Cape May. Steve replied, "Helll nooooo! You'll do more damage at the dock than you will out there."

I'll tell you one thing about Steve; he knew how to handle weather. One time, Tedd Prat was running the *Anna*, and he had a load of four hundred wooden bear traps aboard her back. Tedd called Steve on the sideband radio, frantic. It was blowing 100 knots steady, and they took a sea so bad it shifted all the four hundred traps on the boat!

Steve told him, “Sloooww doowwn. Sloooww dooowwn. You want speed over ground, not speed over air!”

Well, we were about to be in a superstorm: Eastern and Central US, March 1993. Some called it the superstorm; others, the Storm of the Century. Both names were well-earned. When three independent weather patterns converged in the Gulf of Mexico in March 1993, the resulting storm system caused three days of crippling snow, whirling seas, coastal flooding, blizzards, tornadoes, and bone-chilling cold. The amount of snow and rain that fell during the storm was almost biblical—forty-four million acre feet, comparable to forty days’ flow on the Mississippi River at New Orleans, according to a National Climatic Data Center report.

The superstorm of 1993 was a freak of nature. Its seeds had been sown a month earlier as the jet stream (the river of air that flows east to west thirty thousand feet above North America) dipped dramatically down from Canada and blasted cold arctic air across Montana, Wyoming, Colorado, Kansas, and Texas and into the Gulf of Mexico before banking back up the Eastern Seaboard. The jet stream looked like a giant *U* flowing over the central and eastern United States. On Friday, March 12, a cluster of powerful thunderstorms formed in the northwestern Gulf of Mexico and then merged with a narrow band of snow and rain that was pushing in from the West Coast. The two storm systems collided with the jet stream, and by 7:00 p.m., they began screaming across the gulf toward Florida, pushing a large storm surge ahead of their path.

“The sea conditions were absolutely incredible, unbelievable,” a coast guard petty officer told the *Washington Post.* “It looked like a big washing machine. There were huge waves and spray and hail.”

The sea was so powerful that the two-hundred-foot freighter sank seventy miles off Fort Myers, Florida. Three people were rescued from the fifty-miles-per-hour winds and thirty-foot swells, but seven crew members died when coast guard helicopters ran low on fuel and had to return to base.

“They were just getting the hell beat out of them,” an officer said. “I felt for them. They were just holding on, either too weak to grab the basket or too scared to grab it. We were so close—so close—

to getting these guys, and we did absolutely everything we could. And we couldn't get them."

Ten miles from Key West, a 147-foot freighter hauling M&Ms and candy bars ran aground on a coral reef. Several charter fishing vessels and sailboats sank in deeper seas. By the time the superstorm had passed, the coast guard had deployed more than a hundred planes, helicopters, and boats, rescuing 235 people on more than a hundred boats in the Gulf of Mexico.

The more I think about that trip, I don't think Josie liked me. She was in the wheelhouse being snippy, saying, "You go home in bad weather."

"What are you trying to say?" I asked.

"You offshore lobstermen go home in bad weather. You go home!"

Well, of course, I didn't talk back to the captain. I was taught, if the captain says the moon is green, then the moon is green. I shrugged it off and made a couple big loaves of banana bread, which always picked up the spirits. I make great banana bread.

She put me on watch in the worst part of the storm. I could see the isobars almost touching each other on the weather fax machine. (The lines around high and low pressure on a weather map are called isobars, or lines of equal pressure. When isobars are close together, it is very windy.) The sound of the wind blowing through the mast and wire rigging sent shivers through my spine from the 3/4-inch wire cables attached to the outriggers on the mast. The seas had to be sixty to seventy feet at least, if not bigger. All the wire rigging in the mast sounded like a horrible loud pitch whistle that was an instrument roaring the scream of death that awaited us on the other side of a fifty-foot wall of water, and it seemed like it took forever and a day to climb the raging sea.

I will tell you honestly, besides the fishing vessel *Adventure*, this was the worst weather I had ever been in. I saw Captain Josie's light on in her stateroom. I wasn't sure, but I swear I heard her giggling.

I knew one thing. I wasn't about to knock on her door! I had my hand on the trim button a few too many times. I do admit staring up at those huge walls of seawater, whispering to myself, "Oh shit!"

What an incredible sea boat the *Anna Bo* is in horrible weather. I do admit, being on a one-hundred-foot boat is a lot better than being on a seventy-two-foot vessel, especially with outriggers. (An outrigger is a big metal kite with a heavy weight in the middle forward of the steel kite, and there is one for each side of the boat, connected to a chain and a long beefed-up pole about fifty feet long to help stabilize the boat.)

After the weather subsided, we finished up hauling the lobster gear. Josie made the decision to go see if she could catch some groundfish while the lobster gear soaked for a few days.

It wasn't very successful. All we caught were dogfish and more dogfish. (Dogfish, or sand sharks. The meat is used in England for fish and chips. In America, we call dogfish a trash fish.) We hauled the remaining lobster gear and had one day left of hauling before we headed for the dock.

Josie asked if Sean and I could help her change the oil in the generators. There was a big oil tank with fresh oil that was in the middle of the engine room forward of the main engine. That was Sean's job, getting fresh oil. I was on the port side, helping with the oil filters, while Captain Josie was draining the oil from the generator. Meanwhile, Sean filled the generator back up with oil, and Josie checked to see if it was the right amount and started the generator back up again. Then Josie and I went to the other generator to do the same thing. Sean was getting the oil, and I was helping with the filters. When the other generator started to bog down, Josie hurried over to the stalling generator, and I followed. Josie bypassed the throttle and told me to hold this button and don't let go.

Josie went back over to the other generator to finish the filters, and Sean kept filling the oilcan from the oil tank. The stairs to get out of the engine room were on the starboard side of the boat, where the generator was that Josie was working on. I looked at the gauges on top of the generator that I was holding the button to. They were rattling worse than those outriggers in 100 knots of wind.

My ears started to hurt really badly from the ringing sound in my head. That's when I knew something bad was going to happen! As soon as I took my finger off the button, there was a huge explosion. The explosion blew me right by Sean. I had good sea legs, so I used them to direct my fall toward the engine-room stairs.

As I looked up, all I could see was smoke—heavy, heavy black smoke. Then I thought I saw something coming at me. I was right; it was Sean running for his life. I don't think he saw me. Well, I know now that it's over, and I thought about it.

How could he see me with all that black smoke! Well, he ran right over me. He even used my head as a step, and I could feel the force of pressure from his boot on my head with all his body weight lunging off it. Well, now I feel bad because it wasn't the case of him leaving me there. How in the hell could Sean know I was on the steps? I flew by Sean to the bottom of the staircase, followed by thick black smoke so that you couldn't see one foot in front of you.

Well, I was a fool! I ran up the stairs after Sean. I reached out and grabbed his shoe. As the shoe almost slipped out my hand, I got a shoestring tackle. I caught up to Sean at the top of the staircase and started choking him, asking, "Why did you leave me there?"

He said in a squeaky tone with little air, "I was going to go get the fire extinguisher."

Then Josie came over and started sniffing the air repeatedly. Josie asked, "Do you guys smell flesh burning?"

Sean and I looked at each other, bewildered by what she had just asked us. Then we both slowly looked to see where the whiff of smoke was coming from. Both our eyes followed it to my boot.

That's when I started feeling the pain. A piece of shrapnel from the engine block had ricocheted off a pylon and into my boot. I automatically started jumping around, trying to get my boot off. The piece of shrapnel burned my Achilles tendon to the point where there was a 1-½"-wide by 3"-long second- and third-degree burn to the flesh.

Over the years of being stitched up, broken fingers and so forth, I've accumulated a lot of medical supplies. So for the hell of it, I got some Silvadene from a nurse friend. She said, "Take this. Knowing your job, you might need it someday." She was totally right. Always be prepared for the worst, and pray for the best, especially out at sea where there are no doctors around.

The doctor said I was lucky. Burns get infected very easily without proper treatment. (Silvadene is a solid white cream prescription for burns.)

We stayed and finished hauling the rest of the lobster gear. Josie worked through the night and into the day to finish up. I wasn't mad at Josie at all; any experienced person could have made the same mistake.

Steve should have had two separate pumps to drain the oil out of the generators, to make sure the oil wasn't draining while it was running. But he only had one. Josie forgot to shut one of the numerous valves and buttons in the engine room to shut off the generator that was running. So all the oil was draining while I was holding the button.

Needless to say, I didn't go to Alaska. I did plant 210 tomato plants in the worst drought in decades in my hometown of Plympton, Massachusetts, that summer of 1993, when I was healing up my burn and my mind for that matter.

Our neighbor down the street from my father's house owned seventy-two acres of land. As a child, I'd go through their property to my favorite fishing spot. Dan Shlitz was a horticulturist. He could walk you through the woods and tell you every type of plant and tree as you followed him on a path surrounding his seventy-two acres, which he called Gods country! I learned a lot from this man. He even taught me the benefits of bartering, which I still do to this day. And when I eventually went back out to sea, I kept in touch with him to give him seafood for fresh blueberries, strawberries, and vegetables.

I was finally healed up and ready to go back out to sea and do what I do. I decided to go to another port in Sandwich, Massachusetts. I landed a site with the Colberellas on the *Almare*. It was the first time I'd ever seen a settlement sheet before (a list of boat expenses: fuel, food, bait, gear).

I told Doug Colberellas, "I feel like I'm going through somebody's wallet looking at the settlement sheet."

He laughed. "Yeah, yours!" He couldn't believe I'd never seen a settlement sheet before. Some people say the Howards' settlement sheet is fuel, food, bait, gear, Howard factor, and the fuck factor on top of that.

I'll tell you one thing. I've never and will never find a better pair of employers on the entire East Coast. Doug Colberellas, Lenny Colberellas, and Ted Colberellas are three brothers who started from a skiff selling a five-gallon bucket of lobsters to selling ten thousand to twelve thousand pounds of lobster. Now they own two lobster boats and a scallop boat. They literally worked the flesh off their hands to get to where they are today.

I wish that I'd never left them, but as always, God has a plan for us! As Confucius said, "The first step is the hardest for the thousand-mile journey ahead." I didn't work for them long before a couple of crewmates I used to work with came down from the *Mechelle Le* and asked if I wanted to come back and work with them. The captain has the last say on who gets hired or fired on a boat, but in rare circumstances like this one, if all the men on deck want to work with one particular deckhand? Well, point being, the bottom line is if the captain has a happy crew working like a well-oiled machine, then it's going to happen because the better the crew, the more money they're going to make. And it all comes down to the almighty buck!

Don was the new captain, and he wanted me to work for him. No problem. I worked with Don on the deck of the *Mechelle Le*, and we became good friends. After almost every fishing trip, we would go and get a nice meal to get ready for our cocktail bonanza! I wasn't getting along with one of my mates on the *Al Mar*—or, I should say, he was driving me out of my mind (or what I had left of it anyways).

I took the offer, regrettably, and still am sorry to say to myself, "Well, the first step to a thousand-mile journey is the hardest."

To my surprise, Paul was back on deck. He was the deckhand I made my first trip with. He was just as excited to see me as I was excited to see him. We had a lot to talk about and laugh about too! It's nice to encounter someone you had a traumatic experience with that you never thought you would ever see again your whole life.

He told me he didn't remember the job being nearly as hard as his first trip. I told him, "Maybe because we have wire gear with fifty-trap trawls instead of one-hundred-trap solid-oak wood trawls."

(Everyone started converting to wire lobster traps. They were cheaper and a lot less lighter than the oak wood traps, and wire outlasts the wood traps from a worm that actually penetrates the wood and makes a home while eating it.)

Then I told Paul, "You don't have the Buster threatening to suck your eyeball out!"

Paul laughed. He really respected me a lot for sticking it out with what very few men have done on the *Sea Slave*. The few, the proud, and the stupid. Paul knew what I went through. I look back now and realize that not many people would have put up with all that abuse. Or should I say, very few people would have put up with it at all.

Needless to say, I lasted two years before I needed a change. It seems like the magic number before I had to move on to the next boat. My next move was not very far to jump ship at all. There was another boat that docked next to the *Mechelle Le* at Dicky's Wharf in Hyannis Harbor at Cape Cod, Massachusetts.

The *Liam Bull* boat owner, Roger Cootes, was the founder of the shoal waters to catch lobsters. The shoal waters are twenty-five thousand square miles of ocean where lobsters mate only once a year. Lobsters come from 360 degrees to meet at this spot.

Roger told me the shoal waters are not what they used to be. He said, sadly, when he first found the shoal waters, the lobster trap would be chock-full of lobsters. Then on the outside of the lobster trap, there were lobsters hanging on, and you had to take them off the trap before it even got aboard the boat.

Roger Cootes shared up very fairly on his settlement sheet because he was a very fair man, and he took care of the men that worked for him on his boat.

My oldest sister came to the dock one day and was talking to Roger Cootes. When my sister and I went to lunch, she told me Roger said I was the hardest worker he'd ever seen in twenty-five years. That's how long Roger had been offshore lobstering at that time I was working for him.

I had a lot of fun on that boat. Dave Harvey was in stitches laughing so much! I do admit I was a little out of control. Well, okay. I was a freight train out of control, and I was out of my mind as well for that matter. Chip was one of the hardest captains to work for besides the *Sea Slave*. Chip made you a lot of money, and that was the bottom line.

My first year was hard. Chip tried to get me to quit for a full year. Well, we know that didn't work for the first year.

I remember he was screaming at me like a dog! He was pointing his finger on the ground where I was supposed to stand in front of the wheelhouse door. I liked his spirit; he never gave up trying.

My first trip on the *Liam Bull*, the crew and I were on the stern of the boat, heading out to sea. We were sitting and talking. It was a beautiful summer day overlooking all the sand dunes, leaving the cape to head to the shoal waters for lobster mating season. How do I distinctively remember this beautiful day? you wonder. Why and how?

The two deckhands—Neil Quiply and another greenhorn—wanted me to kill the captain! Dave was sitting on the rail and tapping his cigar ash off, just listening to Neil (deceased) complain on how deeply intolerable Chip was, and he was making their lives miserable.

Finally, Dave said something very calmly. Dave said, "You leave me out of this. Just talking about this is breaking the law."

The reality of the situation was this: that's how miserable Chip had made that crew become aboard that boat until you were back at the dock unloading and heading home. Even then, Dave told me, after greetings with my wife at home, I would go down the cellar to my punching bag with a picture of Chip on it, and I would punch the living crap out of him till my rage would subside.

By the second year, Chip came around. I told Chip one day, watching the line come out of the rope locker, he was getting ready to tell the guy setting the traps. There was a snarl coming so he could get out of the way in time so he didn't get stuck in the middle of the mess and get taken out the stern and dragged to the ocean floor. And he'd probably never be seen again after he was eaten by crustaceans and sand fleas down to the bone.

I told Chip, "That's okay. I was like your new dog. You have to kick it around a little bit before you got to like it." I actually got that miserable prick to chuckle a little bit.

I remember Roger took the boat once, and everybody was at the galley table, complaining about Chip. Deckhand Neil had a falling out with Chip and couldn't wait to vent his opinion. Roger kept making him wait to take a turn to have a poke at Chip. Dave had been with Roger for ten years at the time, and he knew what was going on. Dave didn't care—in one ear and out the other. "Show me the money," he'd say! We had another greenhorn, Adam, have a poke at Chip. Then it was my turn.

Meanwhile, Roger was still telling Neil to shut up. "Wait your turn!" His arms were folded, and he was tapping his fingers on the galley table with a big and impatient sigh!

So I figured I'd toss a wrench in the gears. I said Chip threatened to throw me overboard last trip. "You're lucky you still have a captain to run this boat."

You should have seen Dave's poker face start to crack. He was ready to bust out laughing at any moment.

Finally, Neil got a chance to express his innermost feelings toward Captain Chip.

"Okay, Neil, it's finally your turn. Go ahead," Roger said with his hands on his face, anticipating a laugh.

Neil slapped the galley table with his hand as hard as he could. He then said with a loud cry, "Let me tell you about Captain Creepy!"

I about choked on my tongue, and Dave almost swallowed his cigar. He always was chewing on one.

Roger covered his face with his hands, and his elbows were on the galley table. But I saw him shaking, trying to hide his laughter from Neil, which made me laugh even more. This added to Neil's frustration and anguish.

Captain Chip told Roger I was a literal time bomb waiting to go off. Chip also knew I was as hard as they come. Point being, I was at home using a Victorinox knife to cut some monofilament. (A

Victorinox knife is a little five-inch knife with a red handle that is way too sharp.) I did the unthinkable. I cut the top part of my index finger above my middle knuckle all the way to the bone. The bone actually saved my finger from being totally cut off.

I was supposed to go back out to sea the next day, so I cleaned the cut and taped a Popsicle stick to the bottom of my cut finger. The next thing I did was forget it ever happened. I blocked the fact that I just cut my finger to the bone. I was out of my mind—literally!

It was Easter. I remember Chip laughing to Roger about my big Easter basket full of candy and medical supplies, which my wife gave me to head out to sea with. When we got to the fishing grounds, I knew Chip would not turn the boat around after steaming 180 nautical miles and burning over four hundred gallons of diesel fuel just to get to the fishing grounds.

The next day, I started taping my finger up in the galley. Dave walked over to me as I was sitting at the galley table and looked at all the blood squirting out of my finger. I continued bandaging my finger up for the long day ahead of me, cursing it to stop bleeding. Dave started laughing at me as he started heading up the galley stairs to the wheelhouse.

I heard Chip ask Dave, "What's so funny this damn early in the morning?"

Dave said to Chip, "You'll see." And he walked by Chip to go out the wheelhouse door on deck, chuckling.

Later that week, the cat was out of the bag, meaning Chip saw the cut I went out to sea with. I was at the rail, and I heard Chip talking to Roger on the sideband radio. Chip said to Roger in a really serious and slow tone, "His finger. It needed stitches, Roger." I think it scared Chip, and that's why he severely wanted me off that boat.

Everybody thought I was crazy, and it pissed me off. I didn't think I was crazy.

I remembered a saying my father used to say: "If five people call you a horse, start looking for a saddle." So I went to see a physiatrist to prove to everyone—including my wife—that I was not crazy.

So my wife made an appointment with Dr. Dorosa through a family friend that recommended him. When I went for my first visit to this psychiatrist, I thought he looked like a mad scientist. We sat down in his office, and I asked him if he could tell me if I was crazy or not. I told him, "Everyone thinks I am. I don't feel crazy. Well, I have these attacks."

He asked, "What kind of attacks are you talking about?"

I explained it to him. "When I am working, I'll snap into this different personality or this whacked-out character."

So I explained a scenario to the doctor. In the dead of winter, at the rail, looking for a high flyer in sea smoke. (When the water is warmer than the air, it creates a thick smoke that comes off the ocean.) It is not a pretty sight. It really means you're going to freeze your ass off. The sea spray literally freezes in midair, blowing gusts of winds at 40 to 50 knots. It feels like little needles hitting you in the face. That's after your first cup of coffee at 3:00 in the morning, knowing there is a twenty-hour day ahead of you.

I think of the story about that man who was scared to go on deck in twenty-to-thirty-foot seas sums it up. This job is not for the meek. They say a hard ship builds character. Well, they were right on the money. I've had a few captains ask me, "Who are you today, Kyle?" Decades of being out to sea has hardened me severely.

Dr. Dorosa replied, "It could be the way your mind handled the sleep deprivation and stress of the elements."

I also told him that I'd learned, if you did not have the bad times, you would not appreciate the good times. If it was nice all the time, life would be boring. That's why I especially like New England—the change of season, spring, summer, fall, and Jack Frost. You'd get the winter blues. Then spring comes around and puts new life in you. Like in spring, the first smell of a fresh-cut lawn. Then in the fall, the first smell of smoke from a wood stove taking the chill out of a house. If you did not have the bad times, you would not appreciate the good times. There seems to be a balance in life.

Dr. Dorosa told me that was healthy because one of the highest rates of suicide is the change of seasons. I thought the holidays had the highest rate of suicide, but it did not.

When I came back to the boat to get her ready to go fishing again, Dave asked me how the session with the psychiatrist went. I told him, "Very well. He didn't think I was crazy at all."

Dave slowly took his cigar out of his mouth and said, "He lied to you." And he walked away chuckling.

The two best memories I have out at sea are on the *Liam Bull* and *Mechelle Le*. On the *Liam Bull*, all I remember about that day is why did we go to sleep? It was the end of an eighteen-to-twenty-hour day. We were hauling a trawl, and a swordfish came up looking like Moby Dick with all the line wrapped around it. I was the only one that knew how to clean and slime the swordfish. I didn't mind at all. Then Chip cut the two-to-three-hundred-pound swordfish up, and we froze most of it then put the rest in the fridge. Then the next thing I knew, we were on deck after one and a half hour of sleep for another eighteen-to-twenty-hour day.

The best birthday present I ever got was on the *Mechelle Le*. It was July 7, my birthday, on a hot summer night. I was at the rail, waiting for a trap to come out of the water. I had both hands on the rail of the boat and was leaning my head overboard. I liked watching the needlefish or to maybe get a glance at a mahi-mahi. All of a sudden, this sword came right at my head. A swordfish had gotten wrapped around the ground line. When we hauled the trawl, the swordfish came up headfirst. I moved my face just in time before the sword impaled my head. It was so close, the swordbill of the fish hit the visor of my baseball hat and took my hat right off my head. Then I got slapped in the face with the eyeball of the fish. Its eyeball was the size of a tennis ball. I looked like Sanford on *Sanford and Son* (a TV show for old-timers on TV Land), with my hand on my heart like I was having a heart attack crying out to his deceased wife, Elizabeth, "It's the big one, Elizabeth!"

Another two years on the *Liam Bull* and another step toward a thousand-mile journey! I left after two years. Roger gave me eight hundred dollars for nothing and pointed at the door of the wheelhouse. He said that the door was always open for me to come back.

I heard a rumor the Colberellas bought another boat—the *Miss Luli*, a solid aluminum boat. So I went to investigate in Sandwich,

Massachusetts, in Cape Cod, where the boat was docked. I'd been fishing fifteen years at this time, and I was a freight train going full throttle with no brakes!

I remember, after I got a job on the *Miss Luli*, I was helping the boat get ready to go out to sea. Roger came down to the Sandwich dock to talk to Doug Colberellas about me. All I heard was I was supposed to get a land job, and I was.

Doug Colberellas said, "What is he supposed to do, Roger, after fifteen years of offshore lobstering?"

I've never been on land for a very long time, and over the years—well, I didn't really learn how to adapt very well on land. All I knew was the sea. It horrified me to think about getting caught up in the rat race on land.

After all these years, I've been conditioned to work an eighteen-to-twenty-hour day, and I loved being 180 nautical miles out to sea, away from everybody. Until I had kids. Then it was all heartache every second 24-7 until I got back home to see them again! When you add love to your work ethic, you turn into a raging bull!

That's what I have to come to grips with running away my whole life; it's like one long escape! I honestly tried that day I left the *Liam Bull*. When I drove home after leaving the *Liam Bull*, I felt like it was the longest drive I'd ever been on, and I only lived five minutes away from the boat. A part of me was lost; the sea was my life.

I remember panicking like a caged animal. I ran to the phone like it was the key for the lock on the cage door. As soon as I knew I was going back out to sea that day, I felt calm. All my anxiety went away.

The Colberellas brothers gladly hired me back to work for them.

I loved working on the southeastern part of Georges Bank. There is warmer water, and that meant tropical fish! Summertime was tuna time! I would bring a fishing rod to catch tuna and mahi-mahi for when there was a long steam. Sometimes the boat would be adrift at nighttime to save fuel. (*Adrift* means floating free with the currents and tide, not moving on a boat's own power.) That's when I would fish for squid and baitfish for tuna and mahi-mahi bait.

There was a strict rule when you were on watch at nighttime: never go on deck alone! Falling overboard with everyone sleeping and no one steering the boat—I don't even want to think about that, to be honest with you! When the boat is adrift, I go on deck at night. I told the captain once, if someone falls overboard when adrift, they definitely don't belong on a boat.

There is more mahi-mahi than you can shake a stick at in the southeastern part of Georges Bank. I even caught a wahoo once with an avid rod-and-reel recreational fisherman, Ben Hamilton. (Wahoo is a fish found worldwide in tropical and subtropical seas. It is best known to sports fishermen as its speed and high-quality flesh makes it a prized game fish. In Hawaii, the wahoo is known as *ono*.)

This kid knew everything about trawling, jigging—you name it. One day, Ben Hamilton and I were trawling for tuna fish on the *Miss Luli*, and something really big hit the lure and almost spooled the reel. (*Spooled* means the fish takes all the line on the reel and keeps going until there is no line left on the fishing reel. Not good!)

When Ben finally got the fish close enough to the boat to see the fish, Ben screamed, "Whahoo!"

So I also screamed, "Wahoo!"

Then Ben said, "No, Kyle. It is a wahoo."

So I screamed "No, it's a wahoo!" really loud back to Ben.

When we landed the fish aboard the boat, it was a four-to-five-foot torpedo-looking fish with lots of teeth. It reminded me of a huge barracuda. I asked Ben, "What the hell is it?"

Ben looked at me. He was laughing and shaking his head slowly. Then, softly, he said, "Kyle, it's a wahoo fish."

By wintertime, it was my usual two years on this boat. Time to move and take another big step for my thousand-mile journey. It was a cold February, and I heard another rumor the boat *Mike and Kris* out of Gloucester, Massachusetts, was catching a great deal of lobsters, and the price was very high for them. Ray Chadwick is the owner of the boat. He is a really nice man though kind of a sharp pencil as far as the settlement sheet went. Hence, he had his house painted and put it on the trip settlement. (Trip settlement includes food, fuel, bait, and supplies for the trip. And paint the owner's house!)

Ray Chadwick owned an offshore lobster boat years prior to his boat, the *Mike and Kris*. Unfortunately, a horrible mishap happened! There was a big storm approaching, and a coast guard weather buoy went out of commission for some reason. Ray Chadwick's boat, the *Wind Sail*, got caught in the horrible storm and went down a sea so big that the whole boat actually flipped over itself from going down such a huge and steep sea! How do I know this? Two men miraculously survived and were rescued by the coast guard: the captain and a deckhand. God bless those men!

I heard a rumor that Ray had a nervous breakdown and turned into one of the nicest men you could and will ever meet.

Todd Hamilton is a courageous captain and loyal lobsterman. When the sea blew the windows out of the *Adventure* in November 1987, he stayed by us through the whole storm, even when the coast guard came to get us to tow us home. He asked the coast guard if he could pull up alongside us to say, "Have a happy Thanksgiving."

Unfortunately, Todd left to run his own inshore lobster boat. Ray hired a new captain, and when he saw me, he said, "You still fishing, Kyle?" Captain Cris and I go way back; we worked together on the *Sea Slave*. Then he went to work for Big Bay Lobster Co. in New Hampshire. Well, he's now working for Ray and still is to this day.

Cris liked me, but this boat beat my all-time records. I didn't last two trips on this boat. Why? Let me put it this way. I was taught on my very first trip out to sea. Whatever is said on a boat stays on a boat! Besides, if the captain of your ship says that the moon is green, then the moon is green! Truly!

As a matter of fact, this boat beat my record on the *Twin Ducks* when Patric Brody owned it. This is actually a pretty funny story. Well, at least Lenny Colberellas thought so. I told him the story on the *Almare* while he was lying in his rack. Some fishing boats are set up were the captain sleeps in the wheelhouse or the stateroom is in the wheelhouse. I was on watch, telling him the story, and he laughed for a good while. I think he laughed himself to sleep, to be honest with you.

The *Twin Ducks* was out of Sandwich, Massachusetts, along with the *Almare* and a lot of other lobster boats. I was young and feeling my oats at this time. I think maybe I was full of piss and vinegar, which could be a better way to put it.

I'm finally going to tell the whole truth. It even gets funnier. I was the cook. So I did all the grub shopping at Stop and Shop up the street from the dock. There was a back road—or the long way, I called it. So after grub shopping, I put all the food in my Ford F250 diesel truck.

A friend—well, I'll call him my acquaintance. My acquaintance gave me some pot, and he said, "Careful. It's really strong." I think I was twenty-three or twenty-four at the time. You couldn't tell me anything. I was driving the back way to the boat real slowly, and I took a humongous toke off this marijuana cigarette.

The next thing I know, a cop drives by real slow the opposite way. So I held the hit in until the policeman passed me. I could see the boat right down the street, so I sped up. The next thing I knew, my ears started ringing, and I lost control of the truck. So I figured the safest thing to do was go into the woods with an engine that weighed 3,800 lb. alone.

It went from a bright sunny day to black. My windshield looked like a car wash from the leaves hitting the windshield. I realized my foot was still on the gas, and I let off and rolled to a stop. I got out of the truck, and I was in a jungle. It was so thick with leaves, I couldn't see where the road was! So I pulled, ran, stumbled my way to the light to find the road.

When I found my way back to the road, there were a few onlookers who saw me. Just as they put it, "He drove his truck right into the woods!" Good thing they didn't have hijacking laws back then.

This curious man was driving by slowly to see what the excitement was. I ran up to the car, got in, and said, "Drive me to the boat and hurry." I was yelling at him that I was in an accident.

I remember the horrified look on his face. I saw myself in the rearview mirror. I had leaves stuck all over my face and scratches like a rabid cat attacked me! He said, "You're not going to do anything to me, are you?" I said no. I pointed to the blue boat docked at Louie's

Lobster Mart, where we loaded gear, bait, and food. He kept asking, "Well, where is your vehicle?"

I told him, "It's in the woods somewhere."

When I got near the boat, I jumped out. I ran a football field to the boat. So I was winded when I told Patric Brody that my brakes failed, and I drove my truck into the woods. Patric was a retired easy-going family man. To him, I must have looked like this wild crazy man. I had leaves stuck to my face, scratches, and a torn shirt from briars and branches trying to get out of the woods. I remember him wide-eyed, looking at me like I just killed somebody! Especially after all the rumors he's heard about me already. That poor man! I'm so sorry, Patric Brody! Truly, I am!

So meanwhile, my deck mate drove me to the scene of the accident, telling me he knew everybody in town. He even went to high school with the policeman on duty. The policeman said, "As long as there is not over three hundred of damage to the truck, I won't have to make a police report." The deckhand even knew the junkyard owner and told him we'd be out to sea for a week, and the guy said he wouldn't charge me storage for some lobsters.

The captain asked me what happened. I told him, "My brakes went out on me, and I knew I had to act fast, so I ditched the truck in the woods." He started laughing, walked away, and left. I think he heard the same thing I heard. All fishermen lie except me and you, and I don't know about you!

Meanwhile, Patric Brody went over to the *Almare*. He ran into the wheelhouse shaking like a leaf, telling Lenny Colberellas, "Kyle. Kyle. He-he drove his truck into the woods." The poor man was horrified!

Doug Colberellas told me that Patric Brody sold his boat and got out of this business because of people like me! Well, I am who I am! One captain said to me one day, "Kyle, you can't change a leopard's spots!"

*****

(On the harder side!) The *Mya and Kibbly* went into the shipyard in Gloucester, Massachusetts, for a month to make some needed repairs and painting. There is a huge travel lift that has four three-foot-wide straps that go under the boat the whole length of it, and it lifts the boat out of the water. It then carries the boat to a specific spot in the shipyard to be worked on. This is called dry-docked.

I slept on the boat Monday through Friday and went back home to Cape Cod for the weekend. Then I came back to work on Monday.

Eric, another deckhand, said, "Careful of John." I asked why, and Eric said, "When John drinks, he's an asshole." Eric slept on the boat with John one night, and he pushed Eric into a fire extinguisher and ran away drunk.

John had a real Napoleon complex problem and weighed one hundred pounds wet. (Napoleon complex is a theorized inferiority complex normally attributed to people of short stature. It is characterized by overly aggressive or domineering social behavior, such as lying about earnings, and carries the implication that such behavior is compensatory for the subject's physical or social shortcomings.)

So John and I were staying on the boat. We were having some beers, and he started in on me. I screamed at him so badly, he got scared and ran away. I didn't think anything of it and shrugged it off.

Tuesday went by with the normal painting and scraping. I turned in early to get a good night's sleep. John had brought somebody else with him to settle the score. I don't mind fighting, but at least wake me up first! I took kickboxing for a while, but it doesn't help much in close quarters. I got one good kick in, and the drunken bastard wobbled, and my bare foot took the refrigerator door handle off. That explained my broken middle toe.

John's partner in crime ran off up the galley stairs. I took off after his partner in crime, and the next thing I knew, John had jumped on my back like a spider monkey and was trying to gouge my eyes out. That was when I said to myself, "Kyle, he has thick rubber gloves on. So if I bite his finger, at least I won't get AIDS."

I was almost at the top of the spiral staircase when John went limp and fell all the way down the stairwell. I waited for him to come back up the stairwell but to no avail. So I went back down the stairs to the galley to see why. He was on his knees with his eyes like water sprinklers, screaming over and over, "My finger! My finger! My finger!" Then he looked me in the eyes and ran off up the stairs again. But this time, I was after his ass, and he saw it in my eyes! I ran after that son of a bitch like white on rice, like my mom used to say!

There was a ladder tied to the rail to get down to the ground. Thank God I watched a television program with my late wife! Truly! Well, I was watching a TV program about how a man went to jail for killing a man that broke into his own house! I remembered this as I was untying the ladder to push him to his death! But no. I just hopefully wobbled the ladder enough to make him piss his pants!

By the time the fight was over and all was said and done with, the galley looked like somebody had cut a chicken's head off and let it loose. There was so much blood everywhere, with trails of blood drops leading to the galley and to the ladder and all over the ladder back into the wheelhouse and down the staircase and back into the galley again! I'm saying there was blood all over the place! Truly!

I cleaned up most of it before daybreak. Poor Ray Chadwick. He was horrified enough after I had cleaned up most of the blood. I couldn't imagine him seeing all the blood before I cleaned up some of it! Ray wanted to call the police, but I insisted he not do that! I said, "I'll handle the matter on my own!"

I still remember the captain scoffing at me when I asked for a five-hundred-dollar advance. So off I went—another big step for a thousand-mile journey with a broken middle toe. But they didn't leave me with a broken spirit!

When I was working on deck earlier on the *Mya and Kibbly*, a fishing mate told me he was headed north to work for Shiffer and Shiffer. He said this company owned seven lobster boats at the time that were fishing in the Gulf of Maine, right on the border of Canada: the Hague line. (It is the North Atlantic boundary between the US and Canada's fishing waters as determined by the World Court in The Hague, Netherlands.) He said to me one day, "Kyle, I've seen more lobsters than you could ever imagine in your wildest dreams."

One day, he did call me and put the captain on the phone. The captain said, "I heard you are looking for a site." Almost in disbelief, he asked, "Have you really been an offshore lobsterman for seventeen years?"

In the year 2002, I had been fishing seventeen hard years at the time, and I fished the Gulf of Pain, as they called it. Why? Because the Gulf of Maine has no mercy whatsoever! The point being? I'm talking about being in twenty-to-thirty-foot seas. And when the crest breaks and falls into the troth, all you hear is a loud noise of freezing sea spray hitting the seawater like an orchestra of icicles in numerous amounts, making a noise that sounds like cold death is on its way! Truly!

I said to the captain, "I've only been an offshore lobstermen for seventeen years now."

He laughed aloud and said, "Well, if you've been a lobsterman for seventeen years, I want you here on my boat!"

I told him I had a broken middle toe, and there was nothing I could do for it except hop up and down the rail.

He said, "Don't worry about it. We're leaving in a few days." The captain told me where to go the night before to stay at a hotel, and my fishing mate Trevis, who got me the site, picked me up and brought me to the boat.

The name of the boat was *Jeffery Rebel.* She was eighty-five feet long and twenty-two feet wide—a hell of a sea boat. Actually, besides the *Anna Bo*, for the size of the *Jeffery Rebel*, it's the best sea boat I've ever been on.

The captain, Nat, had that engine at full throttle. We were plowing into heavy seas with that huge bow of hers going right through those huge cold brick-shithouse seas like nothing! Whoever designed these vessels outdid themselves as an avid boat builder.

Now I know why everyone was so jealous of this Shiffer and Shiffer. He owned seven offshore lobster boats in 2002 and had the whole Gulf of Maine to himself, which was a true gold mine! It was also the coldest and hardest fishing I had ever experienced! It all comes down to how much mental pain, physical pain, and emotional pain you are capable of enduring in the dead of winter with a major cold blast from the north that freezes your piss instantly as it hits the steel bait checker. Then you have the cherry on the sundae with a captain screaming at everyone or anything all day long and all night long. It was truly no joke!

Football is a violent sport. There's no denying it. When two-hundred-pound men, running at speeds of fifteen to twenty miles per hour, smash into each other, it can produce almost a ton (two thousand pounds) of tackling force. That's a lot! And yet we watch. There is just something about it. We watch. Maybe it's the glory of being an athlete. Or maybe it's the special awe of a man who, in the midst of an injury, wills his body to the field and drags himself physically, mentally, and emotionally through a game that he has no business playing. He should be on the injury list, yet somehow, he's pulled himself up from the bowels of his soul to fight for victory—to fight for his team.

We revel in macho stories of heroism because warriors are revered. Warriors are remembered. Warriors may not always have a weapon, but they ultimately say, "Here is something I love and hold dear: my family, my faith, my country. You are the enemy, and you will not hurt what I love without going through me!"

Warriors fight physically, emotionally, mentally, and spiritually for something greater than themselves. They don't always understand the consequences, but they simply know they must fight. They want to win, but they are dedicated to the fight. There is no victory, so warriors place themselves at risk in order to have a chance.

But we just watch. We feel the urge and inkling of the warrior inside, but we have become accustomed to watching. The adrenaline rush from watching our team win seems to satisfy the eternal call. Our TVs and smartphones deliver the perfect placebo that feeds our internal hunger. We are able to watch the war, but we have become less willing to fight it.

And yet the war still takes place all around us. Our families are under attack. Our values are being threatened subtly and violently. Ask yourself the question, "What am I willing to fight for?" There's a battle, and it's for your heart, your life, your family, and your values. This battle is for everything, and the devil plays for keeps.

This is your call! You feel it. You seek to satisfy it. God made us that way because he knew we would have to fight. Now it's time to equip myself as a man, as a father, as a leader, as a warrior. Don't mess with the best because the best don't mess!

Drake Shield was a fill-in captain for Nat to run the *Jeffery Rebel* for one trip only. Captain Drake ran one of his fleet of lobster boats for six years in the Gulf of Maine working for Shiffer and Shiffer. Drake also worked in Alaska, king-crabbing in the Bering Sea in Alaska for years also. To my surprise, he told me he thinks it's colder in the Gulf of Maine than in Alaska. Drake thinks in Alaska, it's a dry cold; and in Maine, it's a wet cold.

Well, I never fished in Alaska, so I can't personally tell you the difference. But I will tell you, in midwinter, after being on deck all day, under my foul-weather gear, my sweatpants would be frozen solid from my sweat busting my ass, lugging those solid oak wood bear traps around all day and night.

Captain Nat was rough around the edges, but he respected me for the hard worker he had on his deck. You only need three men on deck because the captain has a hauling station that makes it possible to steer the boat and haul the lobster gear outside the wheelhouse on deck at the same time. The captain hauls the gear, rails the traps, and watches out for rogue waves for his men on deck—if you're lucky to have a captain that cares enough.

I know for a fact that one of the reasons why I'm still alive today writing this is because of what I always said, "Think of the danger while things are running smoothly!" I always told myself, "The second trap is going to go out the stern before the first trap I'm holding on to is." There were many times that happened, and I'd say to myself, "Whoa! I almost just died." And there was that beautiful Jack Frost chill running up the center of my spine with cleats on his feet!

The first trip was a rough one; 90 percent of the gear was solid oak wood bear traps. I couldn't believe they were still around, and there were air hoses connected to a one-hundred-pounds-per-square-inch air compressor. It came with a two-inch hollow stainless steel nail gun, a one-and-a-half-inch stainless steel nail gun, a one-inch stainless steel nail gun, and a small three-quarter-inch stainless steel staple gun to staple the twine mesh back onto the wood so lobsters couldn't escape out of the trap.

I finally found out why they had brand-new and old solid oak wood traps. Shiffer and Shiffer had men building them on his huge property that included his bait business, catching and selling his own bait to his own boats. Incredible—capitalism at its best! This man had a huge monopoly on lobster boats, making money hand over fist like a faucet with both valves wide open!

I had used nail guns before, but it's been years since I'd used them. I had the two-inch nail gun in my hand, getting ready to shoot the bait rubber back on. The captain was in the line of fire. (Bait rubber is a used piece of tire cut to a strip three inches long and one inch wide. When nailed to the middle of the top part of the trap, the rubber makes a good holder for the bait bags with string. You wrap the string around the rubber, and it holds the bait bag in the middle of the trap, right in front of the entrance to the lobster trap.) I didn't think I would miss and hit him, and I really didn't want to take the chance, so I put my hand, cupping it in the line of fire.

The nail gun misfired twice, sending two two-inch ribbed stainless hollow nails into my palm where the thumb connects to the hand. Only about a quarter inch or less of the nail heads were sticking out of my glove. I looked quickly to see if anybody saw what I did, and no one noticed. Then I grabbed the two nails with my right hand and pulled, but they didn't come out. So I tried it again but with a very composed quiet yet angry pull.

After I successfully pulled the nails out of my hand, the captain turned around and looked at me. The captain asked me if I just shot myself with the nail gun. I said yes and I already pulled the nails out. I thought I had a good poker face, but he must have seen the look on my face—that of a man that had just shot himself with a nail gun! Then again, I wasn't playing poker. I was getting shot with two-inch nails also.

He stopped hauling and made me take my glove off to see, as if he didn't believe me. He looked at my hand and said, "No shit!" He laughed and went back to the hauler to finish hauling the gear. He was laughing out loud with his face toward the sky.

Right there, I knew I had gained a lot of respect from the captain. Captain Nat knew that gun was on one hundred pounds per square inch. That's a lot! Nat told me horrible stories about men who shot those two-inch nails right through a knucklebone, and their hand would swell up like a balloon. And others shot their hand into the oak wood. Then you would have to get the hammer and pry the nail out of the oak wood or pull the nail through the hand.

The next day, Captain Nat asked me how my hand was.

I told him, "My hand will be fine. I was lucky it was a meat shot, and it was not my lobster-banding hand. I'm double lucky!"

Nat put his coffee back in the coffee holder so he didn't spill it from laughing at me. He knew who he had working for him, and he absolutely loved it!

As usual, he pushed me to see what I was made of. Every captain I have ever worked for did this, and as usual, I blew all their minds. Any boat that I'd ever worked for will never forget a worker like me! You might think I'm not sure of myself, or maybe it's safe to say that I got hit in the head too many times! Or maybe it's safe to say I hit myself in the head too many times!

When we got to the month of November, I couldn't believe my eyes! I had only seen one trawl my whole life that did nine hundred pounds, and that was on the *Anna Bo* off Cape May, New Jersey, in March 1993. There was not only one trawl that caught this many lobsters but thirty trawls with fifty traps a trawl: 1,500 traps in total. One trawl filled a fifty-five-gallon barrel full of lobster, eight stackable lobster totes were full (two stacks four high), and the banding table was chock-full of lobsters that were crawling all over the bait in the bait tank. I lost count after well over five hundred lobsters. At a three-pound average, it was well over fifteen hundred pounds of lobster out of fifty lobster traps. There are no lobster shortages in the Gulf of Maine. I'll tell you this much firsthand!

The winter of 2003 on the *Jeffery Rebel* was the most brutal fishing I ever did! Nat wanted to get a Christmas bonus. He would not get it if he landed the boat to unload the lobsters. He needed seventeen thousand pounds more of lobster to make his quota to get a Christmas bonus.

The first cold front came through and gave us two feet of ice hanging on the mast. We continued working through the second cold front, which happened to fall on Christmas week!

I've never spent Christmas out to sea before but for well over one thousand dollars a day. He didn't have enough lobsters. He wanted to go for a bonus, so we went to fix the clear view in Rockland, Maine, and broke the ice off the mast. (The clear view is a special window built in the shape of a circle, and it spins as well. It is heated to keep the sea spray from freezing.)

When we were at Rockland shipyard, the windchill was thirty to forty below zero. The captain rented a car; then he brought us to the laundromat to do our laundry.

I needed some more gloves, and there was a gear store two miles down the street from the laundromat. A lady told me that while she was doing laundry; her husband was also a fisherman.

The gear store was actually right on the way to where the captain was going: Walmart. Now if you were going right by a store, and you had to walk two miles in windchill factor of thirty to forty below, wouldn't you say to yourself, "Sure, I'll give you a ride."

Well, I told the captain the same thing. The gear store was two miles right down the street. It was kind of cold to walk.

The captain looked at the clock. He said, "Fine. Be back here in a half hour. The boat's going to be ready to go fishing!"

The lady that gave me directions asked me, "Is that your captain?"

I said, "Unfortunately."

She said, "What an asshole."

I guess it is true. You will find the true character of a man by giving him a little power.

This was going to be the biggest challenge ever! All I had were blue Hycron gloves that were only rubber and a little bit of cotton on the inside that wore off after only a few trawls. The largest size they make are 10s. I have gorilla fingers from splicing line my whole time being a lobsterman on boats.

When we left Rockland Harbor, we were in the thick of sea smoke.

There are several types of fog (Encyclopedia Entry):

- Sea smoke forms when a light wind of very cold air mixes with a shallow layer of saturated warm air immediately above the warm water. It is usually not very high, and look-outs on ships can usually see over it, but small boats may have very poor visibility because the fog is confined to the layer of warm air above the sea.
- Advection fog is a type of fog that forms surface contact of horizontal winds. This fog can occur with windy conditions. Warm, moist air blows in from the south, and if there is snow or cool moisture on the ground, it will come in contact with the warm, moist winds. This contact between the air and the ground will cause the air blowing in to become cool. Then dew point rises and creates high humidity and forms fog.
- Radiation fog forms when all solar energy exits the earth and allows the temperature to meet up with the dew point. The best condition to have radiation fog is when it had rained the previous night. This helps to moisten up the soil and create higher dew points. This makes it easier for the air to become saturated and form fog. However, the winds must be light (less than fifteen miles per hour) to prevent moist and dry from mixing.
- Precipitation fog forms when rain is falling through cold air. This is common with warm fronts but can occur with cold fronts as well (only if it's not moving too fast). Cold air (dry at the surface while rain is falling through it) evaporates and causes the dew point to rise. This saturation forms a fog.
- Steam fog is a type of fog that is commonly seen in the Great Lakes but can be seen on any lake. This forms during the fall season. As summer ends, water temperatures don't cool right away, but air temperature does. As a mass of dry cold air moves over a warmer lake, the warm lake conducts warm, moist air into the air mass above, and this trans-

port between the lake and air evens out. This corresponds to the second law of thermodynamics, and this law states that "any two bodies that come into contact, the system will become equilibrium state." Steam fog does not become very deep but is enough to block some of the sunlight.

- Upslope fog forms adiabatically. *Adiabatically* is the process that causes sinking air to warm and rising air to cool. As moist winds blow toward a mountain, it glides up, and this causes the air to rise and cool. The cooling of the air from rising causes it to meet up with the dew point temperature. Fog forms on top of the mountains.
- Valley fog forms in the valley when the soil is moist from the previous rainfall. As the skies clear, solar energy exits the earth and allows the temperature to cool near or at the dew point. This forms a deep fog so dense, it's sometimes called tule fog.
- Freezing fog occurs when the temperature falls at 32 degrees Fahrenheit (0 Celsius) or below. This fog produces drizzle, and these tiny droplets freeze when they come into contact with an object. But at the same time, there is sublimation going on. (Sublimation is the transition from the solid phase to the gas phase without passing through an intermediate liquid phase. This endothermic phase transition occurs at temperatures and pressures below the triple point.)
- Ice fog is only seen in the polar and arctic regions. Temperatures at 14 Fahrenheit to 10 degrees Celsius is too cold for the air to contain supercooled water droplets, so it forms tiny ice crystals.

The third cold front came upon us as we left Rockland Harbor! I was midship behind the wheelhouse. Some sea spray hit the steel lobster tank. It literally froze instantly; the seawater didn't even have a chance to drip down. The water hit the tank horizontally, and it froze horizontally. I couldn't believe we were going back to the Gulf of Maine. We risk our lives for what? The root of all evil: money!

The day we left, it was early morning. Everything was frozen solid. I had the deck hose tied to a fifty-five-gallon drum, and I filled it with frozen blocks of redfish. The water temperature in Rockland Harbor, Maine, was 33 degrees. Salt water's freezing point is 28 degrees Fahrenheit. There is definitely a different breed of lobster in the Gulf of Maine. I looked in the lobster tank, and the lobsters were crawling around in 33-degree water temperature like 42-degree water in the supermarket.

This was going to be the biggest challenge I had ever had to deal with my whole life. I knew I had a very strong mind, but when I saw the sea spray freeze instantly as it hit the cold steel, my thoughts weakened a little bit. But the thought of my child opening the refrigerator with no food in it horrified me, and my heart grew so much that it squished all my weakened thoughts right quick and out of my head, as the Mainers say!

You can overcome anything with love in your heart. Truly! Love has no match, and it is the conqueror of everything and everything!

During my watch, I cooked a lot of pasta and rice for the next day. The best and quickest way for a burst of energy is a big spoonful of peanut butter. I knew I would burn up whatever I ate within an hour. I would literally eat and be hungry after one trawl. I could feel my body burning up the food like a roaring fire chewing on the logs of wood like candy.

One of my deck mates, Dave, on the *Liam Bull* said to me once, "You work like an animal, you have to eat like an animal."

The first day, the windchill was fifty below zero with freezing spray. It was blowing a gale (thirty-five to forty knots), and the freezing spray felt like little needles hitting you in the face. It definitely was not a day for the weary fledgling. That is for damn sure!

The first trawl of the morning, I would look around at all the ice buildup on the rails (which was over two feet thick) and wonder, *What the fuck am I doing here?* Then the first trap would come up out of the cold black water chock-full of lobsters, and then I would snap back to reality. After seeing all the lobsters, I'd forget about the freezing needles and the bitter cold wind biting my face.

I also figured out how to deal with the glove situation. As long as I put a dry pair of gloves on every trawl, my hands didn't look like a baboon's ass, so I kept a rotation of nice dry gloves throughout the day. It actually worked out to be a better advantage for me because I could band the lobsters a lot faster. The other deckhands were wearing these huge thick blue winter gloves with a one-inch pile liner inside of them. Believe me, I would have had them too if the son of a bitch gave me a ride to the gear store. Somehow, through my hard experiences, I've learned a better way—the harder way! Like my dad told a group of schoolteachers in the hallway.

"So where is Kyle going to college?" one of the teachers asked.

My dad said, "Kyle is going to the school of hard knocks." And he walked away, laughing.

The next morning, the forecastle had about two inches of water all the way forward on the deck. I thought to myself, *That's odd. The water is supposed to go aft to the drain holes and then to the bilge to be pumped out of the boat when the bilge alarm sounds off.*

The water was from condensation from all the heat we were putting in the forecastle, galley, and wheelhouse.

It was very early, and I was groggy. I did my usual morning routine, stretching my back faithfully every chance I had. I looked at my back like it was my bread and butter. I took care of my back very well, stretching as much as possible.

A lot of guys, after they got to know me well, admitted I was a little off-the-wall. They'd watch me lying on my back, all contorted on the deck, groaning with pleasure from the stretch. I will tell you this much. When I got up in the morning, all I would hear was "My fucking back is killing me!" or "my legs, neck, arms, ass." That's all I remember hearing every morning. Except for the first day. It was usually "Man, am I hung over!"

I remember one day on the *Adventure*, I was so miserable of everybody complaining at the galley table. For breakfast, I had a raw onion peeled, and I was eating it like an apple with a can of sardines at 3:00 a.m. in the morning. I've never seen a galley clear out so quickly in my life. The scary part I remember about the whole thing was that I actually enjoyed it more with a little pickled horseradish and some Mug root beer.

I liked mornings with Captain Nat. He would have a fresh pot of French vanilla mixed with Irish cream every morning. Nat would let us have a coffee or two with my usual six packs of oatmeal and banana with a little cream dolloped on top. I distinctly remember the look on Nat's face. He was very deep in thought, and I knew him well enough not to talk to him first thing in the morning either.

When I got up from the galley table after having my coffee and oatmeal, I noticed all the ice hanging off the overhead almost halfway down the wheelhouse windows. That's when I put two and two together—why the water in the forecastle was not draining aft. My heart started to sink even more when Nat looked at me. I saw nervousness in his eyes! Nat still didn't say a word. It was a moment when we both knew, just from eye contact, what was going on and what we should have done but didn't do: break the ice off the boat!

The ice was so heavy on the mast that the bow of the boat was actually getting pushed underwater. Deep down, I knew we should have broken some ice off the mast the day before. I guess we were ass deep in lobsters and didn't realize it. I didn't know, but I did care!

My first order from Captain Nat was to go get the ice mallets out of the fishhold.

I remember I was talking to a boat architect about how much a boat should roll back and forth. Well, he said when the mast is in the middle or center of the horizon, the mast should have a 1,001-second roll to port and back to the center of the horizon again. The same thing for the starboard roll: a 1,001-second roll then back to the center of the horizon. I wish I had never asked the architect that question! It's so true in life. Sometimes you're better off not knowing what's going on in certain situations.

In this certain fuckup (which is what I called it), the boat had a 1,003 roll. To give you an idea how much ice buildup we had on one pipe on the mast, a pipe structure on the mast had about six inches in girth. I measured over three feet of ice buildup around the lower end of the mast. The middle of the mast had two and a half feet of ice on it. The farther you went up the mast, the less ice there was. The sea spray didn't really reach all the way to the top like it did on the lower part. There was still a good six inches on the base of the antennas and on the very top of the mast above the crow's nest (a platform fixed near the top of the mast of a vessel as a place for a lookout to stand).

I heard one of the deckhands say, "The ice. It's not breaking!"

The ice was like cement. We had pounded the hell out of it for hours on end. I could barely hold the ice mallet after we basically got the crap kicked out of us by the ice! We got what ice we could get off the mast, and then we had a coffee and lunch with a quick change of clothes to go back lobstering again. We earned our money that day and night for that matter.

Captain Chip of the *Liam Bull* told me something one day while I was watching the line for a deckhand who was setting the lobster traps out the stern. I didn't like Captain Chip's perspective on what offshore lobstering does to oneself. Chip said to me sincerely, "Kyle, this job makes you hard, nasty, and mean." He continued, "Look at you, Kyle. You have so much salt in your veins, I bet when you take a shit, your asshole puckers!"

Dave even admitted it too. We were looking for high flyers with ice built up all over our mustaches and eyelids. We were standing in the cold with freezing spray for hours on end that seemed like days, looking for a high flyer and a huge orange ball. I've seen many of the men just snap because they just couldn't take it anymore! Ron Howard, the owner of the *Sea Slave*, used to scream that a lot: "I can't take it anymore!" He was making fun of a greenhorn who couldn't take it anymore!

Now that I think about it, I can't believe Ron acted so tough. We were groundfishing for hake, cusk, cod, halibut, and the occasional haddock! This was a trip from hell. Ron took all his lobster gear out of the water for the winter. He decided to go hook fishing for the winter instead. It was almost two weeks before he decided to maybe wrap the trip up. We went through ten thousand pounds of mackerel in cut-up pieces. We were setting twenty-five hundred hook sets—two sets a day. Mackerel have tiny bone splinters (that's what I call them). You can barely see them, but you sure can feel them in your hand!

Everybody would wait for an experienced pair of hands at the galley table, meaning your hands were seriously calloused. The bone splinters would not penetrate your hands. I've seen hands so sore that they actually waited for someone to open a new box of cereal.

Everybody wanted to go home badly, and Ron knew it. It was the last day, and we were on the last set. I didn't hear Ron say "loose fish." *Loose fish* was when a fish fell off a hook into the water, and it floats to the stern. Because the boat was in gear moving forward, we couldn't really walk to the stern. So when he said "loose fish," you would run your ass off to the stern of the boat. Then you would grab a gaff that was waiting for you and gaff the loose fish.

Well, obviously, now I know why he was so miserable. He almost lost his $1.2 million boat that year. So he decided to take it out on me! He told everybody, "We're going to make one more set. Kyle missed the fish and didn't hustle fast enough."

Well, Ron did turn the crew against me and then some. I thought I was going to get stabbed. Seriously, the crew was pissed!

At the end of the set, the crew came to their senses. They realized Ron was trying to turn them against me and apologized to me!

I still offered to put the fish in the hole. It was the suckiest part of the day! You literally had to lift totes of fish that weighed 200 to 225 lb. each. We would wash the fish in baskets tied to the rail, take a fish pick, and sort out all the different kinds of fish. (A fish pick is a piece of wood one foot long and one inch thick. And on the end, there is a huge thick steel needle about five inches long.) We would catch an average of twenty-five hundred pounds a set at two sets a day. That equaled to a very sore back by the end of the day. You literally would lift five thousand to six thousand pounds of fish by yourself. Talk about getting a strong back!

I was down to the last two totes of fish to be put down the fish hole. Well, I found out years later that Don put a fish pick in the pen board gaff holder. The fish picks didn't belong there because when somebody straddled the pen boards like I did, you can get a big five-inch needle in the calf!

Well, there was a tote on the other side where I was lifting the fish totes. So I asked Don to help me lift it over the pen boards. After he helped me, I decided to slide the tote on the pen boards to the hatch cover so I didn't have to lift the tote twice. When I did, I felt a really bad sting in my right calf. There was a two-by-one-inch rubber hose tied to the pen boards. It was made to hold a ten-foot gaff. The fish pick was only one foot long. All that was sticking out was the pick at the top of the rubber base.

The two-hundred-pound tote that I was sliding helped push the five-inch fish pick all the way into my calf. It must have missed my bone, thank God. When I pulled the fish pick out, I could feel my boot filling up with warm liquid.

Ron told me, "Shut the fuck up, you pussy! And get ready to haul back."

He didn't even let the baited hooks soak like we usually did. Usually, we would let the gear soak, go eat something, change our clothes, and get a cup of coffee.

We hauled the gear back. To my surprise, we caught some fish. I was so mad, I used to fantasize about ways to torture Ron.

Now it was Tim's turn. Tim had this bright idea to sharpen both sides of his knife. The first thing I told Tim when I saw him sharpening his double-edged sword was "You're gonna stab yourself."

Well, Tim had a fifty-pound cusk on the gutting table. When he put the knife in the fish's gut to cut up to the gills, the fish turned, and the knife went into the palm of his hand. I was behind Tim when he did it. All I heard was "fuck!" really loud. Every time he said *fuck*, a huge squirt of blood shot over his shoulder.

To my surprise, Ron came out of the wheelhouse. He looked at Tim's hand and his eyes rolled back into his head as if he was going to faint. He turned right around and went marching into the wheelhouse. I couldn't believe Ron almost fainted. That's when I knew he was a spineless coward!

My calf didn't feel so bad after seeing that blood squirt three or four feet over Tim's shoulder. He had hit something bad; it wasn't good at all!

Clark said we had to stop the bleeding, and Ron agreed. Before they went into the wheelhouse, Clark was screaming for the electric tape. Don and I stayed on deck. We finished hauling back and stowed the fish away.

I'll never forget the pain Tim went through in the forecastle that night going home 180 miles at nine knots. Tim's palm was all taped up and looked all right. Then, all of a sudden, his hand started to swell. You could actually see his hand blowing up. We didn't know why either. He wanted to take the bandage off, but Clark said no. Clark and I were looking through the medical book. I remember Clark stopping at the chapter about when a person is going into shock. Tim had all the symptoms of someone going into shock.

He ended up in the hospital for days with a serious infection. The doctor said we should have taken the bandage off and let it bleed, to let the foreign particles in his hand expel all the toxins.

Well, that year with Ron, I made a whopping $15,000, and the IRS was wondering why I didn't pay my taxes that year! I really didn't make a lot of money in this business except the boats at Shiffer and Shiffer that made up to $125,000 on deck. The captains were making over $200,000 in nine months out of the year. I averaged the better part of eight months out to sea a year, so if I spent thirty years fishing, I spent twenty years out to sea and ten years on land. It's like being incarcerated of your own will: I made my own prison.

I had set a goal to have thirty years on deck—the most I know of anyways. There are fishermen that have fished longer than that on deck. I haven't met or heard of anybody that has been offshore lobstering on deck for thirty years. That's insane!

Usually, after ten to fifteen years, you hear about knees giving out or backs hurting and so forth. Well, I'm going to keep my work attitude the same as always. Okay, men! Let's go to work and work the flesh off our bones to go back to our homes!

I think when I get thirty years on deck, it will be time to become a captain. I often wonder, *Who in the hell is going to hire a madman?* Everyone thinks I'm crazy as a loon, and most of them think I'm certifiable. Sometimes it's better not to think at all. Just concentrate on getting through one lobster trap at a time!

That first year with Shiffer and Shiffer was okay, but the second year totally sucked! Nat had left the *Jeffery Rebel* for good after running the boat for five years. I don't even know if I have it in me to write what I really want to say. I've never been more disgusted my whole career being an offshore lobsterman my thirty years doing it.

I'll tell you one thing: working in fifty to sixty knots of wind and twenty-to-thirty-foot seas for forty lobsters out of fifty traps is not my idea of fun. Taking eighteen hours to haul six trawls, you'd think you were high or something! Maybe when I was younger, I used to love days like that. I will admit, if there were five hundred counts instead of forty counts of lobster, I would have been smiling from ear to ear.

After my third year, I made a good move, and I abolished all my ideas of moving north after what I had experienced and seen! One thing I am adamant about is that whatever happens on a boat stays on a boat! Who knows? Just because I got a bad taste in my mouth doesn't mean I might not go back one day. I feel like one of those disgruntled employees. I let it go and gave it up to God—the one of my only and best friends I'd ever had in thirty years of fishing—as well as my wife and children.

People took my kindness for a weakness until I revealed the true sea dog and scared the fuck out of them!

It's funny. I look back at the low self-esteem I used to have of myself when I was working in Gloucester, working on the *Mya and Kibbly*. There was an experienced deckhand on the dock that was working on the *Mechelle Le* at the time: Ken Poria (deceased). I asked him if the captain and the deckhands on the *Liam Bull* were talking bad about me. He laughed out loud and said, "Hell no. You're a fucking legend. Don't you know that?"

That's when I realized. I guess I made a name for myself.

My father told me, "If five people tell you you're a horse, start looking for a saddle."

One time, my brother Antonio and I were working together on the *Adventure*. This was before Captain Crunch was there, looking for his chest of gold! The captain's nickname was Bingo. They called him that because when a trap came up full of lobsters, he'd say, "Bingo!" He told Antonio and me that we were very humble. It was interesting to him because he saw it in me. Then when my brother came fishing, he saw it in him too.

The other time, I was on the old *Miss Luli* with a marine that had served for twenty-one years. I had to stack the whole trip because, basically, nobody wanted to stack, and I didn't care because my percentage of the catch would be higher. I was on the stern, stacking a trap, and I heard the marine say, "Kyle's very humble."

I remember telling my brother Antonio about it. To my surprise, he looked at me and said, "Look how we were brought up, Kyle." I thought I saw a tear in his eye. We didn't talk about feelings at all. The only feelings we felt or talked about were when we were reeling in a nice trout or mahi-mahi fish that we caught.

I heard a rumor that Ron's boat *Mechelle Le* was going to be on the Discovery Channel, so I called Ron to see if I could make some fishing trips on his boat. Ron said, "Yes, no problem. As long as there are no problems with you."

It was a humbling move on my part because the deck boss on the *Mechelle Le*, Jack, was a young tyrant. A deckhand before me—Ken Poria (deceased), an experienced lobsterman—had enough of Jack, who was a new deck boss at the short time Ken was there. Jack had no respect for anyone, including Ken. Finally, Ken had enough of Jack. He grabbed Jack by the head and brought him down to the scupper (a square hole in the hull, right were the deck is to let seawater go back overboard after taking a wall of seawater on deck). Ken held Jack's head there until a big wave hit the scupper and flooded Jack's nose and ears, and I'm sure he was spitting some seawater out of his mouth as well.

Then after the fishing trip was over, Jack was bickering with Ken about the hundred dollars he owed him that hadn't been paid back yet, and Jack demanded the hundred after the trip was over. After they unloaded the lobsters off the boat and were ready to leave to go home, Ken hopped on the dock and told Jack, "Hurry up if you want your hundred bucks."

As soon as Jack got on the dock, Ken grabbed Jack's ear and literally dragged him to his vehicle while listening to him cry out,

"I don't want the hundred dollars! My ear, my ear, my ear!" He was crying all the way to Ken's vehicle.

I would have loved to make some popcorn and watch that over and over again, belly laughing. When someone pushes my buttons on deck, I tell them all my buttons are broken except one, and it goes *tweeek tweeek tweeek*, ready to break or snap!

I went for the trip with the Discovery Channel with success. I didn't throw Jack overboard, nor did I lose my temper. But once, I had a vision of actually picking him up off the deck, walking in the stern of the boat, and throwing him in the prop wash. That thought left my mind quickly when I thought about what would happen to him if I did that. (Prop wash is the disturbed mass of air or water pushed aft [or forward when in reverse] by the propeller of an aircraft or propeller-driven watercraft. The byproduct of thrust produced by a propeller.)

When I finally watched the Discovery Channel show one year later, I learned how sharp a pencil Ron really has. Point being, the narrator on the show was telling everyone how much each boat made at the end of the trip. The crew I was on made five thousand dollars, and the crew on the *Liam Bull* made ten thousand dollars at the end of the trip.

As soon as I heard that news, I knew where I wanted to work next. After Roger Cootes hired me back to work on his boat, the *Liam Bull*, Dave asked me if the rumor was true.

I asked, "What rumor?"

Dave took this cigar he was always chewing on out of his mouth and asked me a question. He had heard I bit someone's finger off and spit it overboard. It reminded me of my preschool teacher when she made us kids get in a big circle. Then the teacher whispered something in a student's ear and said "pass it on" until it eventually got back in a full circle to the teacher. When it did get back to the teacher, I remember her screaming and laughing out loud with her face to the ceiling. It was a good lesson for me to learn, so I decided to teach everyone a lesson myself.

When I had the incident on the *Mya and Kibbly* and bit John's finger because he was on my back like a monkey trying to gouge my eyes out. The rumor when I got back to Cape Cod, Massachusetts, from the state of Maine was I bit a deckhand's finger off and spit it overboard, so I went with it. My father asked me, "Would you rather be feared or loved?"

After making my first trip back on the *Liam Bull*, I felt like I doubled my share. Then I realized that I did. I called Roger Cootes once to see if he made a mistake on my check. It was for eight thousand dollars, and I only worked a little over a week for it.

Roger Cootes laughed and asked me how it felt to be screwed on all the hard work you did. He was—and always will be—the best owner, captain, mentor, and lobsterman on the whole fleet. He pioneered this industry as far as I'm concerned. Roger Cootes found the lobsters in the shoal water where lobsters come from all over 360 degrees to mate only once a year, when the female lobster molts and her pheromones are set off to trigger all the bigger breeder males. And I mean BIG! And they come marching on in at full force too!

I have a picture of a twenty-nine-pound lobster stuffed and mounted on a beautiful polished oak plaque with a finish lacquer so shiny, you can actually see yourself when you're looking at it. Captain Ron saw me almost get ready to throw a twenty-nine-pound breeder lobster overboard that was at least over one hundred years old. I told Ron that the knuckle on the lobster had a crack in it, and it would die if I put it in the live well.

Ron stopped hauling the lobster gear, looked right at me, and said, "Kyle, if you throw that lobster overboard, I'm going to fire you!"

So I put the lobster in the twenty-thousand-pound live well only to find it dead after we unloaded the boat. Ron gave it to me because I wanted to give the lobster its last rights.

The owner of the *Liam Bull* knew that I was a train wreck waiting to happen. He pulled me aside one day and said, "Kyle, if you don't start making a list every morning what you should be doing for the day, you're going to die."

I heeded his warning and still to this day make a list of what I have to do every day. And if I don't finish the list, I carry it over to the next day.

Jack, the deck boss on the *Mechelle Le*, got sent to Rhode Island to work for the Palatoes. (Basically, that's where you go fishing when no one else wants you on their boat anymore.)

I heard another rumor that a boat owner bought an Alaskan king crab boat and sailed it to Massachusetts. It took thirty-seven days and seventy thousand dollars in fuel to get her there. The *Killame*, she had two sister ships that sank in the Bering Sea. And then they built the *Killame* that lasted twenty years on the Bering Sea in Alaska.

Why do I call it the *Killame*? I have a fishing mate who is paralyzed form the waist down: Harry. I fished with him on deck, and he gave this boat that nickname. And it kinda fits, to be honest with you. Harry has some funny stories and is the most entertaining deckhand I have ever fished with! He had a reply all ready for the comment before you even thought about getting it out of your mouth. I've witnessed deckhands go batshit crazy because of his witty smart-mouth comments that made me spit my coffee out of my mouth from laughing so hard!

Especially Fred. Well, Harry always called him Dead Fred. Why? Because Fred was fifty-five years old and working on deck still. Fred is definitely a tough old sea dog. I'll tell you that much.

One icy cold morning, on the tennis-court-size wooden deck on the *Killame* that was slippery as hell, without ice walkers, you were totally screwed. Dead Fred was taking a piss, and Harry chimed out, "Hurry up, Dead Fred. And take that stent out of your penis and get back to work!"

I thought to myself, *That's it. Dead Fred is going to snap Harry's neck.*

I looked over to see Dead Fred's expression, and to my surprise, Dead Fred was laughing too.

Harry just came to make gas money for his toys back in his garage at home. He had just bought a fifteen-thousand-dollar two-seater four-wheel racing quad that was way too fast. Unfortunately, one of the wheels came off from faulty lug nuts at a very high speed down a narrow path up north in the middle of nowhere. Harry escaped death but snapped his spine, and he was paralyzed from the waist down trying to keep up with that thirst for that big adrenalin rush.

I called the owner for a site on deck. I've worked on and off over the years, and he was always fair with pay as long as you earned it, but he was the most hotheaded boat owner I ever met. The *Mighty Killame* is a great name for her, point being, we were heading into a category 4 or 5 hurricane in the seas from hell!

A category 5 Atlantic hurricane is a tropical cyclone that reaches category 5 intensity on the Saffir-Simpson Hurricane Wind Scale, within the Atlantic Ocean to the north of the equator. They are among the strongest tropical cyclones that can form on earth and have one-minute sustained wind speeds of over 137 knots, or 158 miles per hour. The United States National Hurricane Center currently estimates that a total of thirty-six tropical cyclones between 1851 and 2020 have peaked as a category 5 hurricane (National Oceanic and Atmospheric Administration (NOAA)).

My wife really didn't like this man. I remember pulling the phone out of her hands when I picked up the phone and she heard his name. Full-blooded Irish do not mess around and are no joke! The hand-knit Irish sweaters are handmade by the fishermen's wives for a reason. Each sweater is handmade with its own pattern so the wives can identify the bodies that wash up on the beach from lost fishermen at sea. I can't even imagine the thoughts the wives were having, knitting those sweaters for their husbands. I didn't blame her one bit for pulling the phone out of my hands. The only reason she didn't hit me with the phone was because the kids were in the same room and saved their dad's ass that evening.

The owner should have called the crew's families like all the other boat owners did out of respect for the families—to let the wives and children know when the fathers would be home. Maybe even a short message, if needed, would be sent to a deckhand to ease his mind so he can keep his mind 110 percent on his job so he doesn't die for the day.

Well, he didn't. And it didn't surprise me one bit that he didn't either.

Now this is the fucking worst weather I never want to see again as long as I live! True to that! True to that! All I kept thinking about in my mind was a picture of the steel wave-break flattened like a steel pancake aboard the *Adventure* in the glorified same old saying: "Oh, the price will be high before Thanksgiving holiday."

Here we go again but in the most horrible conditions I could possibly ever imagine and worse! The only reason we made it that trip was because of the *Mighty Killame*! That double-hulled beast went through a sea taller than her stack, and that's at least eighty feet in the air from the waterline easy. The sea was so big that seawater went down the stack and over the main engine. The main engine didn't stall like it did on the *Adventure*. She kept going through the sea like a battleship! That's exactly what that vessel is—a battleship turned into a fishing vessel. It truly was the only reason the crew and I are here to speak about it.

Not like the *Killame*'s two sister ships and the two crews aboard those fishing vessels lost out in the Bering Sea of Alaska. Then they built the *Killame*, a battleship that lasted twenty years on the Bering Sea. I wish the boat could write a book about her life at sea. I can just imagine the seas that challenged her huge double-hulled bow literally pounding through over eighty-foot rouge waves enough to make a greenhorn fall to the deck in the fetal position and start sucking his thumb while pissing himself! True to that! True to that!

I knew something was up when the relief captain, Mario, told me the second rumor was true about a lobster boat that had twenty-five miles of the Hague Line, the best sets in the whole fleet.

(Hague Line—The North Atlantic boundary between the U.S. and Canada fishing waters as determined by the World Court in the Hague, Netherlands (National Oceanic and Atmospheric Administration). A compromise North Atlantic boundary line dividing Georges Bank and its resources between the United States of America and Canada has been drawn by the World Court in The Hague, Netherlands. The new boundary between New England and Nova Scotia gives part of the bank to Canada for the first time. The issue was settled 12 October 1984, and the decision was enforced as of midnight, 26 October 1984. Both Canada and the United

States had agreed to a fourteen-day grace period to allow fishing vessels from both sides to return to their respective sides of the new boundary. The heart of the issue—which has been a source of dispute since 1976, when Canada and the United States extended their eastern boundaries—was control of an area of between thirteen thousand and eighteen thousand square nautical miles that included the northeastern half of Georges Bank, one of the world's richest fishing grounds. The area may also contain oil and gas reserves. The United States had argued that it was entitled to a boundary line that retained all of Georges Bank. Canada had asked for a line dividing the bank virtually in half, leaving all of the northeastern segment under its control. The World Court, in essence, split the difference, setting a line that cut Georges Bank about midway between the two claims. According to the National Oceanic and Atmospheric Administration, which has jurisdiction over fisheries out to two hundred miles off the US coast, including the Georges Bank area, the new boundary will make management of Atlantic fisheries, including cod and haddock, very complex, and will require close consultation with all interested parties. High seas rights pertaining to the area, such as freedom of navigation, are not affected. The Court, at the request of Canada and the United States, established a special chamber of five judges to hear the case, and had considered extensive written and oral submissions presented by both sides during the previous two years.)

Mario only made one trip on the Killame when it happened with an owner with an indispensable amount of money! No worries on old lobster gear that was so old, the trap became a restaurant feeding them. Then they would literally crawl out of the trap through a huge hole in the side. I was all in, and Mario was just as excited as I was to be part of this historical lobster season ahead of us, and that meant we needed a crew like a well-oiled machine.

The *Diana Girl* is the perfect boat for moving lobster gear. She's a hundred feet long and forty feet wide, shaped kind of like a really fat torpedo and all deck. Mario nicknamed her "the big elephant." The chilling system could keep up with one hundred thousand pounds of product in the live well at forty-two degrees—the optimum temperature for a lobster to sustain any length of time in a holding tank out to sea or on land.

Captain Mario was a screamer, and I mean SCREAMER! The longer the trip, the louder he would scream. All you would see when you looked up at the huge glass window box was Mario screaming into the microphone like an enraged madman full of rage with veins sticking out of his head and neck and his face glowing red. He looked like his head was going to explode at any moment!

One day, I was so enraged at Captain Mario, I punched the foam life ring, and I missed hitting the steel wall only to have more rage on top of rage with a boxer's break. When I got home from the trip, my wife called me over to the computer that was in the living room so she could keep an eye on the kid's activity and monitor what was on the computer. When I saw what my wife had looked up, I was shocked. It was maritime law, and the fine for punching a captain is $10,000. It's a $10,000 fine if the captain punches me in the face.

I actually pondered breaking his jaw. It takes up to three months to heal a wired jaw. That is plenty of time for Mario to think about why he screamed at me like he did.

One of my best trips was with Mario catching over forty thousand pounds of lobster, and he paid everyone, experienced or inexperienced. That was just the right ingredient needed for making a disgruntled deckhand. Mario said the secretary made a mistake and that he would look into it. I decided to get a printout of what I made for the year, and it was ten thousand dollars short. And when Mario looked at it, he said, "That is not right. It's way off."

The secretary almost got fired from finding paperwork stuffed in cabinets. She claimed she was starting to get dementia and saved her job.

I was having really bad thoughts of killing my captain. Truly, I would think of different ways to kill Mario until I felt bad for him. Then it would start all over again the next day, and I would be thinking of a new foolproof way to dispose of his body overboard to let the sharks rip him apart limb by limb. And hopefully, his head would be last so he could feel every damn tooth that sank into his flesh! Oooohhhh, that thought put tingles up my spine right to the top of my skull! Truly! That's when I knew I had to move on before I did something very regrettable for the rest of my life.

The owner had another boat built and ready for fishing by this time, so I parted ways with this mad screamer for another step to a thousand-mile journey. The name of the new boat was *Celebrity*. It's a really comforting feeling when you're out to sea two hundred miles and one mile deep to the bottom of the ocean floor with a new purring engine.

One of the deckhands got fish poisoning so bad, a red line started to make its way up his arm. Once you see a red line moving up your arm, you only have maybe a couple days before the red line travels to your heart, and then you die. (Bait poisoning is a serious matter. One of the hazards of handling bait is that bones or sharp fins can puncture the skin, which is the body's first line of defense against infection. I've seen lobstermen with the telltale red streaks up their arms—signs of spreading infection that requires hospitalization with intravenous antibiotics. It's the hazard of this industry.)

Well, in this deckhand's case, the captain had to bring him to the hospital as soon as possible before the red line made it to his heart. Then the captain was responsible accounting for the deckhand's death.

After we got back to the dock and took the deckhand to the hospital, the captain called the accountant to get check advances for the crew. After the captain got off the phone with the accountant, he pulled me aside and told me, "The owner doesn't understand and has no problem with you, but the accountant said she will call the police if I show up at the office."

One thing I've learned over the years is if someone is very guilty about something, the first sign is a major self-defense.

The boat was going to leave the next day, so I decided to stay on the boat for the evening while the other deckhands went on their own elsewhere. I decided to start the evening off right by buying a lot of whisky, and I mean a lot of it. By the time the bottles of whisky were almost gone, I was feeling very disgruntled.

The first thing I looked at was the four-slice toaster perched in the corner, touching the refrigerator. I punched the four-slice toaster so hard, I turned it into a two-slice toaster with a perfect mold of my fist embedded in its side.

Then I got a great idea. I opened the silverware drawer and grabbed a steak knife and proceeded to stab the cabinet that was in front of me so many times, I lost count. I also had a problem with the new head door sticking, so I decided to unstick the door by kicking it in so hard that the door and frame went flying into the wall behind it. When I walked into the head, I was surprised at how cool it looked as I replayed in my mind the door and frame flying off into the wall. That got me even more excited, so I punched the vanity mirror and put my fist right through it.

Out of good faith, I decided to put the doorframe back in place. So I went to the engine room to find the biggest wrench I could find in the toolbox. I found a big crescent wrench that weighed at least three pounds to bang the finish nails back into their rightful place. It worked great except when I missed the nail, it left a good half-inch-deep indent in the wood trim. I calculated the damage to see if it was sufficient for my redemption. I actually got a good sweat out of it, pounding the fuck out of the doorframe for at least a full forty-five minutes or more, and it felt so gratifying walking around the galley and head, assessing the damage I had done.

The next day, we headed back out to sea, and I was securing the deck when the owner's nephew came out and asked me what happened to the toaster. I looked him square in the eyes and said, "Bad weather last trip."

He burst out laughing and walked back into the wheelhouse and shut the door behind him. Nothing else was said to me after that, and the captain even put the vanity mirror on his credit card for me when we got back to the dock. The captain knew why I was disgruntled for my acts of retaliation.

I heard a rumor the Killame was making bank with big trips, and I couldn't resist heading into fall with bad weather on its merry way. It's nice to be on a seaworthy vessel, being very comfortable in bad seas on a hundred-foot vessel rather a seventy-foot one.

I was only on my third trip, and my whole life changed horribly. The owner made a very bad decision to buy a fiberglass ladder and try to use it out at sea. It was very close to the end of the fishing trip when I got on the fiberglass ladder, and it snapped, going into the rope locker (where all the line goes from the lobster trawl). This particular rope locker, you could put up to fifteen miles of line. That's 750 traps and fifteen miles of line piled up all in numerical order down in the rope locker.

In this particular incident, we were only moving five trawls. Flake two miles aft in the rope locker, flake two miles forward, and then I was to come out of the rope locker and let the last trawl drop straight down. Seemed easy enough. We were pulling up to the fourth trawl, and I had to climb down the twenty-foot-deep rope locker to flake the last trawl forward. The deck below me had an I-beam and the deck was clear.

As soon as I got on, the ladder stood up straight. I heard a loud snapping noise, and I fell, landing in the fetal position sideways right below my butt cheek on my thigh muscle. I couldn't move my lower body for ten or fifteen seconds. I was in a blind rage and finally stood up and growled as loud as I could (or maybe a primordial scream is more like it). I finished flaking the last trawl, and I finally got out of the rope locker with a shorter ladder. It was just tall enough to make it out and grab the short ladder to remove it from the rope locker also.

The other deckhands let me just sort the crustaceans for the rest of the trip, seeing how I was injured. The last day was very hard for me to work the deck. But I never quit on deck before, and I was not about to start either. I was always taught to be strong and never give up!

When we got back to the dock and unloaded the rock crab and lobsters, I couldn't control my bladder and pissed myself. One thing I do know is this job is not for the meek. There are and always will be bumps and bruises to be had in this industry. All the captains I had worked for know what I'm made of and always took care of me—point being, I'd taken a bad hit out at sea. Take a trip off with pay then go back out to sea like nothing happened.

Well, this injury is the worst I've ever endured my whole career being out to sea. I finally got diagnosed seven months after the fiberglass ladder snapped. I finally found a doctor that knew exactly what I had: pudendal nerve damage. But the only way to prove it 100 percent is to stick this three-inch needle into my rectum to give me an EMG exam.

EMG (electromyography) and nerve conduction studies are used to help diagnose a variety of muscle and nerve disorders. An EMG test helps find out if muscles are responding the right way to nerve signals. Nerve conduction studies help diagnose nerve damage or disease.

The test came back as pudendal nerve damage, which is very rare. Only one in a hundred thousand people have it, and true cases like mine are even rarer. (Pudendal nerve damage is long-term pelvic pain that originates from damage or irritation of the pudendal nerve—a main nerve in the pelvis. The pudendal nerve supplies areas including the area between the buttocks and genitals [perineum] and the area around the anus and rectum.)

I was with a cane and had incontinence for over one year of intense physical therapy before I could put the cane away. Then I had two more months of work-conditioning physical therapy until the first cold front came in and crippled my pelvis nerve so badly, they stopped after one full month and put the other month on hold. I was the only person to walk through the doors of South Coast Rehabilitation Center with this nerve damage, and they didn't know what to do with me. They didn't want to damage me more, so they called the pelvis guru with thirty years' experience in dealing with pelvis injuries. It took the pelvis doctor over two months of visits to get my incontinence under control again, where I didn't have to buy any Depends (men's and women's incontinence underwear).

Commercial fishing remains one of the most dangerous jobs in the nation, with a fatality rate that is twenty-three times higher than for all other workers. Vessel sinkings account for half of all fishing fatalities; second is falling overboard. These are deaths that are largely preventable.

Considering I've spent thirty years and the better part of eight months out at sea, I'm lucky just to be sitting here, writing this down on paper. I'm here for a reason. I know this now and truly believe it down deep in the bowels of my soul. I lost my wife, I lost my mother, and I lost my father. I felt like I lost my children dual parenting with my sister-in-law. My dog died. It was the last connection, my daughter said, to her mother. Being hurt with permanent nerve damage, this was my first time living on land in thirty years for the better part of eight months a year. I feel like I'm living out a country Western song in real life.

The only reason I endured all of this is from the Bible and Bible study. My pastor for over forty years went to Bible college, where he met his wife. They have seven children together.

The Bible taught me the right way to live. The Bible is a manual for how to live your life with the truth and only the truth. I have a new captain now, the master on his ship for my journey, for the first step is the hardest for eternity!

*****

My brother and I went to the school of hard knocks. I've seen my brother whipped with a dog chain. That reminded me of stories that went back to the biblical times with Jesus! I look at the seventeen-year-old teenagers today and I tell them, "When my brother was your age, he hitchhiked to California twice by the time he was seventeen. From Massachusetts to California is thirty-five hundred miles. That's fourteen thousand long-ass miles to hitchhike, I'll tell you that much! As usual, a lot of them can't conceive it. I like to use the word *fathom*. It fits better!"

If anyone can get anything out of this book, I'd like it to be never give up, only be strong and very courageous. When you come to the end of your rope, tie a knot and hang on for dear life like my seventh great-grandmother taught me. To find out what's wrong with a man, start out with his grandmother on his father's side. The old-timers had only one way—the hard way! Believe me. If I can do it, anybody can do it! I hope someone will read this book and it changes their life like it changed my life. I know I'm as soft as a grape, but now my hardened heart is too.

God gave me some time off to find him. When you are cornered with nowhere to go and in your deepest pain that cripples you, that's when you will find your strength. It is in your weakness as you become closer to God. It's so true, it's scary! My way was a road of pain (self-inflicted). I knew no other way. I walked a lonely road—the only one I knew!

I've surrendered myself to God, which I thought I'd never do in a million years. I have a peace of mind I never had in my whole life. Yes, I've done and said things that I regret, but I'm not that person anymore! I try to look at that person like a stranger, and while I'm not yet what I want to be, praise God I'm not what I used to be. Now I even have a purpose, and I know I have a lifetime of learning to do. Only my seed has been planted, but it's going to grow into a huge 350-foot redwood tree with roots beyond imagination, and no windstorm will ever knock me down!

I know I have a lot to learn and far to go, but instead of thinking how far I have to go, I say to myself, "Look how far you have come!" I have a new journey, and the first few steps are the hardest for this thousand-mile journey to get to eternity. But in the end, I'll be rewarded beyond my wildest dreams!

Philippians 4:6–8 states:

> Don't worry about anything but everything by prayer and supplication with thanksgiving let your requests be made known unto God. And the peace of God, which surpasses all understanding, shall guard your hearts and minds through Christ Jesus.
>
> Finally, brothers and sisters, one last final thing. Fix your thoughts on things that are true, honest, right, pure, lovely, whatsoever things that are admirable, think of things that are excellent and worthy of praise.

Printed in the USA
CPSIA information can be obtained
at www.ICGtesting.com
LVHW051338051224
797944LV00001B/3